LAND O LAKES

Cookie COLLECTION

CRESCENT BOOKS

Recipes developed and tested by the Land O'Lakes Test Kitchens.
Recipes © 1990 Land O'Lakes, Inc.

MONOPOLY® game equipment, page 62, used with permission from Parker Brothers
© 1935, 1985.

Photo credits: Sanders Studio, Inc., Chicago, IL

Library of Congress Catalog Card Number: 90-61070
ISBN 0-517-03307-0

This edition published by:
Crescent Books
Distributed by Outlet Book Company, Inc.
A Random House Company
40 Englehard Ave.
Avenel, New Jersey 07001

Manufactured in USA

Pictured on front and back cover:

1. Cinnamon Sugar Crispy (page 9)
2. Lemon Meltaway (page 56)
3. Teddy Bear Cookie (page 29)
4. Toasted Pecan Toffee Bar (page 26)
5. Lace Cookie Cups with Ice Cream (page 79)
6. Cherry Scotchie (page 33)
7. Fruit Filled Thumbprints (page 56)
8. Peanut Buttery Cookie (page 57)
9. Tropical Orange Coconut Drop (page 10)
10. Jan Hagel (page 48)
11. Citrus Pie Bar (page 51)
12. Cherry Date Skillet Cookie (page 13)
13. Honey of a Cookie (page 67)
14. Banana Cream Sandwich Cookie (page 58)

15. Orange Butter Cream Squares (page 84)
16. Cookie Jar Cookie (page 22)
17. Chocolate Pixies (page 71)
18. Buttery Butterscotch Cutout (page 72)
19. Buttery Jam Tart (page 25)
20. Spiced Molasses Cookie (page 67)
21. Half-Hearted Valentine Cookie (page 91)
22. Peanut Butter Chocolate Chip Bar (page 30)
23. Crisp 'n' Crunchy Almond Coconut Bar (page 36)
24. Favorite Butter Cookies (page 61)
25. Pecan Tartlets (page 80)
26. Cherry Date Sparkle Bars (page 36)
27. Chocolate Chunk Cookie (page 30)

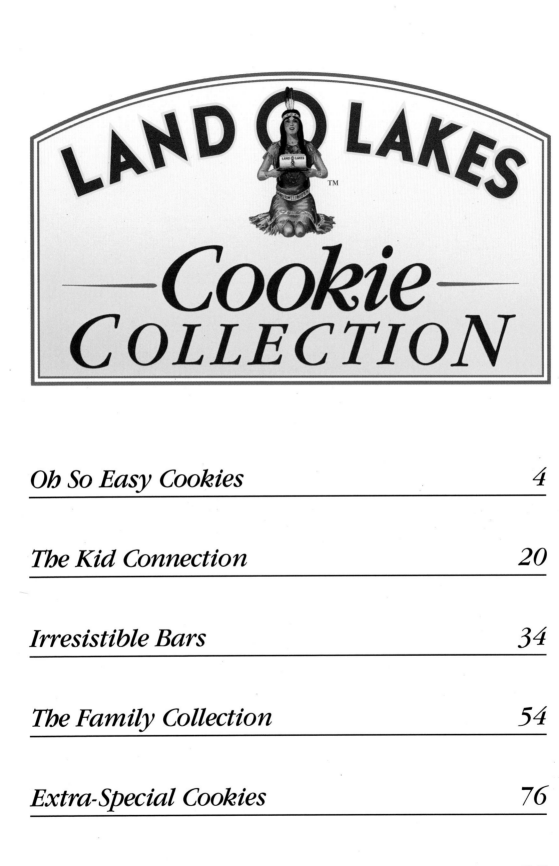

LAND O LAKES
Cookie COLLECTION

Oh So Easy Cookies   *4*

The Kid Connection   *20*

Irresistible Bars   *34*

The Family Collection   *54*

Extra-Special Cookies   *76*

Index   *95*

Oh So Easy Cookies

The cookies in this chapter are great for the novice or busy baker. Each recipe has 10 or less ingredients and can be made in a short amount of time. Included are pat-in-the-pan bars, easy-to-roll balls, slice-and-bake and drop-from-a-spoon cookies. Just measure, mix, bake and enjoy.

Pictured here are: Cinnamon Sugar Crispies, page 9, and Layered Chocolate Butterscotch Bars, page 6.

SOUR CREAM CHERRY BARS

Cool and creamy—these cherry bars are topped with crunchy almonds.

Crust
2 cups all-purpose flour
⅔ cup sugar
⅔ cup LAND O LAKES® Butter,
    softened

Filling
1 can (21 ounces) cherry fruit
    filling
¾ cup dairy sour cream
2 teaspoons almond extract
¾ cup sliced toasted almonds

Heat oven to 350°. For crust, in large mixer bowl, combine all crust ingredients. Beat at low speed, scraping bowl often, until mixture is crumbly, 2 to 3 minutes. Press on bottom of ungreased 13×9×2-inch baking pan. Bake for 20 to 25 minutes, or until lightly browned around edges.

For filling, in medium bowl, stir together fruit filling, sour cream and almond extract. Spread over hot crust. Sprinkle nuts over top. Continue baking for 15 to 20 minutes, or until edges are bubbly. Cool completely. Cut into bars. Store, covered, in refrigerator.

Makes about 3 dozen bars

LAYERED CHOCOLATE
BUTTERSCOTCH BARS

The variety of textures and flavors—vanilla wafers, coconut, chocolate, butterscotch and peanuts—is sure to please.

2½ cups crushed vanilla wafers
¼ cup LAND O LAKES® Butter,
    melted
2 teaspoons vanilla
1 cup flaked coconut

1 cup semi-sweet chocolate chips
1 cup butterscotch chips
1 can (14 ounces) sweetened
    condensed milk
½ cup salted peanuts

Heat oven to 350°. In small mixer bowl, stir together vanilla wafers, melted butter and vanilla. Press on bottom of greased and floured 13×9×2-inch baking pan. Sprinkle coconut, chocolate chips and butterscotch chips over top. Pour milk over top; sprinkle with nuts. Bake for 20 to 27 minutes, or until edges are lightly browned. Cool completely. Cut into bars. Store, covered, in refrigerator.

Makes about 3 dozen bars

Sour Cream Cherry Bars

Swedish Coconut Cookies

SWEDISH COCONUT COOKIES

A Scandinavian heritage is the foundation for this buttery, tender cookie.

3½ cups all-purpose flour
2 cups sugar
2 cups LAND O LAKES® Butter,
  softened

1 tablespoon baking powder
1 teaspoon baking soda
1 teaspoon vanilla
1 cup flaked coconut

In large mixer bowl, combine flour, sugar, butter, baking powder, baking soda and vanilla. Beat at low speed, scraping bowl often, until well mixed, 3 to 4 minutes. Stir in coconut. Divide dough into halves; shape each half into a 12×2-inch roll. Wrap in waxed paper. Refrigerate until firm, at least 2 hours.

Heat oven to 350°. Cut rolls into ¼-inch slices. Place 2 inches apart on ungreased cookie sheets. Bake for 9 to 14 minutes, or until edges are lightly browned. Cool slightly; remove.   *Makes about 8 dozen cookies*

CINNAMON SUGAR CRISPIES

These tender buttery cookies are rolled in cinnamon and sugar for a crisp cookie. A pecan in the center makes them a little more special.

Cookies
  2 cups all-purpose flour
½ cup sugar
1 cup LAND O LAKES® Butter,
    softened
1 egg
¼ teaspoon baking soda

¼ teaspoon salt
2 teaspoons vanilla

Sugar Mixture
¼ cup sugar
½ teaspoon ground cinnamon
36 pecan halves

Heat oven to 375°. For cookies, in large mixer bowl, combine all cookie ingredients. Beat at low speed, scraping bowl often, until well mixed, 2 to 3 minutes. Shape rounded teaspoonfuls of dough into 1-inch balls.

For sugar mixture, in small bowl, combine sugar and cinnamon. Roll balls in sugar mixture. Place 2 inches apart on greased cookie sheets. Place 1 pecan half in center of each cookie. Bake for 10 to 14 minutes, or until edges are lightly browned. Remove immediately.

Makes about 3 dozen cookies

TROPICAL ORANGE COCONUT DROPS

Moist coconut and a touch of orange add tropical flavors to these rich butter cookies.

2 cups sugar	1 teaspoon salt
1 cup LAND O LAKES® Butter, softened	1 teaspoon vanilla
	1 teaspoon orange extract
3 eggs	3½ cups all-purpose flour
1 teaspoon baking powder	½ cup flaked coconut

Heat oven to 350°. In large mixer bowl, combine sugar, butter, eggs, baking powder, salt, vanilla and orange extract. Beat at low speed, scraping bowl often, until well mixed, 1 to 2 minutes. Stir in flour and coconut until well mixed, 2 to 3 minutes. Drop rounded teaspoonfuls of dough 2 inches apart onto greased cookie sheets. Bake for 8 to 12 minutes, or until edges are lightly browned. Remove immediately.   *Makes about 5 dozen cookies*

LEMON DOODLES

Crisp on the outside and chewy on the inside—the lemon flavor adds a new twist to ever popular Snickerdoodles.

2½ cups all-purpose flour	1½ teaspoons cream of tartar
1½ cups sugar	1 teaspoon baking soda
¾ cup flaked coconut	¼ teaspoon salt
1 cup LAND O LAKES® Butter, softened	1 tablespoon lemon juice
	½ teaspoon grated lemon peel
2 eggs	

Heat oven to 400°. In large mixer bowl, combine all ingredients. Beat at low speed, scraping bowl often, until well mixed, 2 to 4 minutes. Drop rounded teaspoonfuls of dough 2 inches apart onto ungreased cookie sheets. Bake for 7 to 10 minutes, or until edges are lightly browned. Remove immediately.   *Makes about 4 dozen cookies*

Tropical Orange Coconut Drops

Cherry Date Skillet Cookies

CHERRY DATE SKILLET COOKIES

Snowy coconut coats these made-in-the-skillet, buttery date cookies.

1 cup LAND O LAKES® Butter
1 cup firmly packed brown sugar
1 package (8 ounces) chopped
   dates
1 egg
3 cups crisp rice cereal

1 cup flaked coconut
½ cup chopped maraschino
   cherries, drained
1 tablespoon vanilla
2½ cups flaked coconut for rolling

In 10-inch skillet, melt butter over medium heat. Stir in sugar and dates; remove from heat. Stir in egg. Return to heat; continue cooking over medium heat, stirring constantly, until mixture comes to a full boil, 4 to 6 minutes. Boil, stirring constantly, 1 minute; remove from heat. Stir in rice cereal, 1 cup flaked coconut, cherries and vanilla until moistened. Let stand 10 minutes. Shape rounded teaspoonfuls of dough into 1-inch balls. Roll each ball in remaining 2½ cups coconut. *Makes about 5 dozen cookies*

GRANOLA GOODY BARS

These chewy and nutritious snacks are loaded with good-for-you ingredients like granola, raisins, almonds and honey.

2¼ cups granola-type cereal
½ cup all-purpose flour
½ cup sliced almonds
½ cup raisins
¼ cup firmly packed brown sugar

½ cup LAND O LAKES® Butter,
   softened
¼ cup honey
½ teaspoon baking soda

Heat oven to 350°. In large mixer bowl, combine all ingredients. Beat at low speed, scraping bowl often, until well mixed, 1 to 2 minutes. Press firmly into ungreased 9-inch square baking pan. Bake for 20 to 25 minutes, or until edges are browned. Cool completely. Cut into bars.
Makes about 2 dozen bars

MOCHA ALMOND BARS

Coffee and almonds give this bar a unique flavor and a crunchy texture.

Bars
2¼ cups all-purpose flour
  1 cup granulated sugar
  1 cup LAND O LAKES® Butter,
    softened
  1 egg
  1 teaspoon instant coffee
    granules
  1 cup sliced almonds

Glaze
  ¾ cup powdered sugar
  1 to 2 tablespoons milk
  ¼ teaspoon almond extract

Heat oven to 350°. For bars, in small mixer bowl, combine flour, granulated sugar, butter, egg and instant coffee. Beat at low speed, scraping bowl often, until well mixed, 2 to 3 minutes. Stir in nuts. Press on bottom of greased 13×9×2-inch baking pan. Bake for 25 to 30 minutes, or until edges are lightly browned.

For glaze, in small bowl, stir together all glaze ingredients. Drizzle glaze over warm bars. Cool completely. Cut into bars.

Makes about 3 dozen bars

COCONUT SNOWDROPS

These snowy-white cookies have tender coconut for a moist chewy cookie.

  2 cups all-purpose flour
  1 cup flaked coconut
  ½ cup granulated sugar
  1 cup LAND O LAKES® Butter,
    softened

  ¼ cup milk
  1 egg
  1 tablespoon vanilla
    Powdered sugar, for sprinkling

Heat oven to 350°. In large mixer bowl, combine flour, coconut, granulated sugar, butter, milk, egg and vanilla. Beat at low speed, scraping bowl often, until well mixed, 1 to 2 minutes. Drop rounded teaspoonfuls of dough 2 inches apart onto ungreased cookie sheets. Bake for 12 to 15 minutes, or until edges are lightly browned. Remove immediately. Cool completely; sprinkle with powdered sugar. *Makes about 3 dozen cookies*

Mocha Almond Bars

Glistening Cherry-Fig Bars;
Snowball Cookies

GLISTENING CHERRY-FIG BARS

These fruit-filled cake-like bars are sweetly studded with figs and cherries and sprinkled with sugar for a glistening top.

1½ cups all-purpose flour
¾ cup sugar
½ cup LAND O LAKES® Butter,
   softened
2 eggs
½ teaspoon baking soda

1 teaspoon vanilla
¾ cup chopped figs
¼ cup chopped maraschino
   cherries, drained
1 tablespoon sugar for sprinkling

Heat oven to 325°. In small mixer bowl, combine flour, ¾ cup sugar, butter, eggs, baking soda and vanilla. Beat at low speed, scraping bowl often, until well mixed, 2 to 3 minutes. Stir in figs and cherries.

Spread into greased and floured 9-inch square baking pan; sprinkle 1 tablespoon sugar over top. Bake for 22 to 30 minutes, or until wooden pick inserted in center comes out clean. Cool completely. Cut into bars.

Makes about 2 dozen bars

SNOWBALL COOKIES

A favorite at Christmas time, pecan-filled Snowball Cookies are scrumptious all year 'round.

2 cups all-purpose flour
2 cups finely chopped pecans
¼ cup granulated sugar
1 cup LAND O LAKES® Butter,
   softened

1 teaspoon vanilla
Powdered sugar for rolling

Heat oven to 325°. In large mixer bowl, combine flour, nuts, granulated sugar, butter and vanilla. Beat at low speed, scraping bowl often, until well mixed, 3 to 4 minutes. Shape rounded teaspoonfuls of dough into 1-inch balls. Place on ungreased cookie sheets. Bake for 18 to 25 minutes, or until very lightly browned. Remove immediately. Roll in powdered sugar while still warm and again when cool. *Makes about 3 dozen cookies*

ALMOND SHORTBREAD BARS

These tender almond bars are perfect with fruit or after dinner coffee.

---

2 cups all-purpose flour
1 cup sugar
1 cup LAND O LAKES® Butter,
   softened

1 egg, separated
¼ teaspoon almond extract
1 tablespoon water
½ cup chopped almonds

Heat oven to 350°. In large mixer bowl, combine flour, sugar, butter, egg yolk and almond extract. Beat at low speed, scraping bowl often, until particles are fine, 2 to 3 minutes. Press on bottom of greased 15×10×1-inch jelly-roll pan. In small bowl, beat egg white and water until frothy; brush on dough. Sprinkle nuts over top. Bake for 15 to 20 minutes, or until very lightly browned. Cool completely. Cut into bars.

Makes about 2½ dozen bars

OLD-WORLD RASPBERRY BARS

This buttery good raspberry-filled bar combines the goodness of Old World baking and updated convenience.

Crumb Mixture
2¼ cups all-purpose flour
1 cup sugar
1 cup chopped pecans
1 cup LAND O LAKES® Butter,
   softened
1 egg

Filling
1 jar (10 ounces) raspberry
   preserves

Heat oven to 350°. For crumb mixture, in small mixer bowl, combine all crumb ingredients. Beat at low speed, scraping bowl often, until mixture in crumbly, 2 to 3 minutes. Reserve 1½ cups of the crumb mixture. Press remaining crumb mixture on bottom of greased 8-inch square baking pan. Spread preserves to within ½ inch of edges. Crumble 1½ cups reserved crumb mixture over top. Bake for 42 to 50 minutes, or until lightly browned. Cool completely. Cut into bars. *Makes about 2 dozen bars*

Almond Shortbread Bars

The Kid Connection

Children will love to eat these cookies and will be eager to help mix and shape the dough. Kids' favorites—chocolate, caramel and peanut butter—play a starring role in this chapter. Bake up a batch and see the smiles light up!

Pictured here are: Teddy Bear Cookies, page 29; Cookie Jar Cookies, page 22; and Peanut Butter Chocolate Chip Bars, page 30.

CARAMEL ROCKY ROAD BARS

Caramel, peanut, marshmallow and chocolate lovers, BEWARE—
these bars may be deliciously habit forming!

Crumb Mixture
1 cup all-purpose flour
¾ cup quick-cooking oats
½ cup sugar
½ cup LAND O LAKES® Butter,.
   softened
½ teaspoon baking soda
¼ teaspoon salt
¼ cup chopped salted peanuts

Filling
½ cup caramel ice cream topping
½ cup salted peanuts
1½ cups miniature marshmallows
½ cup milk chocolate chips

Heat oven to 350°. For crumb mixture, in small mixer bowl, combine flour, oats, sugar, butter, baking soda and salt. Beat at low speed, scraping bowl often, until mixture is crumbly, 1 to 2 minutes. Stir in nuts. Reserve ¾ cup of the crumb mixture. Press remaining crumb mixture on bottom of greased and floured 9-inch square baking pan. Bake for 12 to 17 minutes, or until lightly browned.

For filling, spread caramel topping evenly over hot crust. Sprinkle nuts, marshmallows and chocolate chips over top. Crumble ¾ cup reserved crumb mixture over top. Continue baking for 20 to 25 minutes, or until crumb mixture is lightly browned. Cover; refrigerate 1 to 2 hours, or until firm. Cut into bars.   *Makes about 2½ dozen bars*

COOKIE JAR COOKIES

Coconut, oats and rice cereal will make these crisp and tender cookies a
cookie jar favorite!

3½ cups all-purpose flour
1 cup granulated sugar
1 cup firmly packed brown sugar
2 cups LAND O LAKES® Butter,
   softened
1 egg
1 teaspoon cream of tartar

1 teaspoon baking soda
½ teaspoon salt
1 cup quick-cooking oats
1 cup crisp rice cereal
1 cup flaked coconut
½ cup chopped walnuts or pecans

Heat oven to 350°. In large mixer bowl, combine flour, granulated sugar, brown sugar, butter, egg, cream of tartar, baking soda and salt. Beat at low speed, scraping bowl often, until well mixed, 2 to 3 minutes. Stir in oats, cereal, coconut and nuts. Drop rounded tablespoonfuls of dough 2 inches apart onto ungreased cookie sheets. Bake for 13 to 16 minutes, or until lightly browned. Remove immediately.   *Makes about 4 dozen cookies*

Caramel Rocky Road Bars

Buttery Jam Tarts

BUTTERY JAM TARTS

These cherry-almond tarts are moist, tender and easy to make.

2½ cups all-purpose flour
½ cup sugar
⅔ cup LAND O LAKES® Butter,
   softened
1 egg
¼ teaspoon baking soda

¼ teaspoon salt
2 tablespoons milk
1 teaspoon almond extract
¾ cup cherry preserves
   Sugar for sprinkling

Heat oven to 350°. In large mixer bowl, combine flour, sugar, butter, egg, baking soda, salt, milk and almond extract. Beat at low speed, scraping bowl often, until well mixed, 3 to 4 minutes. Roll out dough, ½ at a time, on well-floured surface, to ⅛-inch thickness. Cut out with 2½-inch round cookie cutter. Place ½ of the cookies 2 inches apart on ungreased cookie sheets. Make small X or a cutout with a very small cookie cutter in top of each remaining cookie. Place level teaspoonfuls of cherry preserves in center of each cookie. Top each with another cookie; press together around edges with fork. Sprinkle with sugar. Bake for 11 to 13 minutes, or until edges are very lightly browned. Remove immediately.

Makes about 2 dozen cookies

TEENTIME DREAM BARS

These are double-deck, twice-baked bar cookies.

Crust
1 cup all-purpose flour
⅓ cup sugar
½ cup LAND O LAKES® Butter,
   softened

Filling
½ cup sugar
¼ cup chunky peanut butter
½ cup light corn syrup
2 eggs
¼ teaspoon salt
½ teaspoon vanilla
½ cup flaked coconut
½ cup semi-sweet chocolate chips

Heat oven to 350° For crust, in small mixer bowl, combine all crust ingredients. Beat at low speed, scraping bowl often, until mixture is crumbly, 1 to 2 minutes. Press on bottom of greased 9-inch square baking pan. Bake for 12 to 17 minutes, or until edges are lightly browned.

For filling, in small mixer bowl, combine sugar, peanut butter, corn syrup, eggs, salt and vanilla. Beat at low speed, scraping bowl often, until well mixed, 1 to 2 minutes. Stir in coconut and chocolate chips. Pour over crust. Continue baking for 20 to 30 minutes, or until filling is set and lightly browned. Cool completely. Cut into bars.   *Makes about 3 dozen bars*

TOASTED PECAN TOFFEE BARS

This delicious bar blends the taste and flavor of a cookie and a candy into one special treat.

Bars
2 cups all-purpose flour
1 cup firmly packed brown sugar
1 cup LAND O LAKES® Butter, softened
½ teaspoon ground cinnamon
1 teaspoon vanilla

¾ cup chopped pecans, toasted
½ cup milk chocolate chips

Topping
½ cup milk chocolate chips
¼ cup chopped pecans, toasted

Heat oven to 350°. For bars, in large mixer bowl, combine flour, sugar, butter, cinnamon and vanilla. Beat at low speed, scraping bowl often, until mixture is crumbly, 2 to 3 minutes. Stir in nuts and chocolate chips. Press on bottom of greased 13×9×2-inch baking pan. Bake for 25 to 30 minutes, or until edges are lightly browned.

For topping, sprinkle chocolate chips over bars. Let stand 5 minutes to melt. Slightly swirl chips with tip of a knife as they melt, leaving some whole for a marbled effect. *Do not spread chips.* Sprinkle nuts over top. Cool completely. Cut into bars.   *Makes about 3 dozen bars*

OLD-FASHIONED BROWNIES

Brownies, a favorite in every family, are quick, easy and delicious.

2 cups all-purpose flour
2 cups sugar
½ cup unsweetened cocoa
1 cup LAND O LAKES® Butter, softened

2 eggs
1 teaspoon vanilla
1 cup chopped walnuts or pecans

Heat oven to 350°. In large mixer bowl, combine flour, sugar, cocoa, butter, eggs and vanilla. Beat at low speed, scraping bowl often, until well mixed, 1 to 2 minutes. Stir in nuts. Spread into greased 13×9×2-inch baking pan. Bake for 20 to 25 minutes, or until firm to the touch. Cool completely. Cut into bars.   *Makes about 2 dozen bars*

Toasted Pecan Toffee Bars

Buttery Caramel Crisps

BUTTERY CARAMEL CRISPS

These thin, crispy graham cracker bars are topped with marshmallows, buttery syrup and lots of almonds and coconut.

12 double graham crackers	1 teaspoon ground cinnamon
2 cups miniature marshmallows	1 teaspoon vanilla
¾ cup firmly packed brown sugar	1 cup sliced almonds
¾ cup LAND O LAKES® Butter	1 cup flaked coconut

Heat oven to 350°. Line ungreased 15×10×1-inch jelly-roll pan with graham crackers. Sprinkle marshmallows evenly over crackers. In medium saucepan, combine sugar, butter, cinnamon and vanilla. Cook, stirring constantly, over medium heat until sugar is dissolved and butter is melted, 4 to 5 minutes. Pour evenly over crackers and marshmallows; sprinkle nuts and coconut over top. Bake for 8 to 12 minutes, or until lightly browned. Cool completely. Cut into bars. *Makes about 4 dozen bars*

TEDDY BEAR COOKIES

Cookies become a special treat when shaped into cute little teddy bears.

1 cup sugar	1 teaspoon baking powder
⅔ cup LAND O LAKES® Butter, softened	¼ teaspoon salt
1 egg	2 squares (1 ounce each) unsweetened chocolate, melted
2 teaspoons vanilla	
2¼ cups all-purpose flour	

Heat oven to 375°. In large mixer bowl, combine sugar, butter, egg and vanilla. Beat at medium speed, scraping bowl often, until well mixed, 1 to 2 minutes. Add flour, baking powder and salt. Continue beating, scraping bowl often, until well mixed, 1 to 2 minutes. Divide dough into halves. Place ½ of the dough in small bowl; blend in melted chocolate.

For each teddy bear, shape a portion of either color dough into a large ball (1-inch) for body, a medium ball (¾-inch) for head, 4 small balls (½-inch) for arms and legs, 2 smaller balls for ears and 1 small ball for nose. If desired, add additional balls for eyes and mouth. Repeat with remaining dough, making either vanilla or chocolate teddy bears or mixing the doughs to make two-tone teddy bears.

To form each cookie, place large ball (body) on ungreased cookie sheet; flatten slightly. Attach head, arms and legs by overlapping slightly onto body. Bake for 7 to 8 minutes, or until body is set. Cool 1 minute on cookie sheet. Remove immediately. *Makes about 2 dozen cookies*

CHOCOLATE CHUNK COOKIES

Chunks of chocolate and walnuts make these chewy cookies extra special.

¾ cup firmly packed brown sugar
½ cup granulated sugar
1 cup LAND O LAKES® Butter,
    softened
1 egg
1½ teaspoons vanilla
2¼ cups all-purpose flour

1 teaspoon baking soda
½ teaspoon salt
1 cup coarsely chopped walnuts
1 milk chocolate candy bar (8
    ounces), cut into ½-inch
    pieces

Heat oven to 375°. In large mixer bowl, combine brown sugar, granulated sugar, butter, egg and vanilla. Beat at medium speed, scraping bowl often, until well mixed, 1 to 2 minutes. Add flour, baking soda and salt. Continue beating until well mixed, 1 to 2 minutes. Stir in nuts and chocolate. Drop rounded tablespoonfuls of dough 2 inches apart onto ungreased cookie sheets. Bake for 9 to 11 minutes, or until lightly browned. Cool 1 minute on cookie sheet; remove immediately.   *Makes about 3 dozen cookies*

PEANUT BUTTER CHOCOLATE CHIP BARS

Two all-time favorite flavors team up in these crunchy bars.

Bars
¾ cup firmly packed brown sugar
½ cup granulated sugar
1 cup LAND O LAKES® Butter,
    softened
1 egg
1½ teaspoons vanilla
2¼ cups all-purpose flour
1 teaspoon baking soda

½ teaspoon salt
1 cup chopped peanuts
1 cup semi-sweet chocolate chips

Topping
1 cup semi-sweet chocolate chips
½ cup creamy peanut butter
½ cup chopped salted peanuts

Heat oven to 375°. For bars, in large mixer bowl, combine brown sugar, granulated sugar, butter, egg and vanilla. Beat at medium speed, scraping bowl often, until well mixed, 1 to 2 minutes. Add flour, baking soda and salt. Continue beating until well mixed, 1 to 2 minutes. Stir in nuts and chips. Press on bottom of ungreased 15×10×1-inch jelly-roll pan. Bake for 12 to 17 minutes, or until edges are lightly browned.

For topping, in small saucepan, combine chocolate chips and peanut butter. Cook over low heat, stirring constantly, until melted, 4 to 5 minutes. Spread over warm bars. Sprinkle nuts over top. Refrigerate until topping sets, about 1 hour. Cut into bars. Store, covered, at room temperature.

Makes about 5 dozen bars

Chocolate Chunk Cookies

Cherry Scotchies

CHERRY SCOTCHIES

These moist and chewy brownie-like bars are filled with lots of cherry and butterscotch goodness.

2 cups all-purpose flour
¾ cup firmly packed brown sugar
½ cup flaked coconut
¾ cup LAND O LAKES® Butter, softened
1 egg
1 teaspoon baking powder

½ teaspoon salt
2 teaspoons vanilla
½ cup chopped maraschino cherries, drained
2 tablespoons all-purpose flour
1 cup butterscotch chips
Powdered sugar, for sprinkling

Heat oven to 375°. In large mixer bowl, combine 2 cups flour, brown sugar, coconut, butter, egg, baking powder, salt and vanilla. Beat at low speed, scraping bowl often, until well mixed, 1 to 2 minutes. In small bowl, toss together drained maraschino cherries and 2 tablespoons flour. Stir in cherries and butterscotch chips. Spread into greased and floured 13×9×2-inch baking pan. Bake for 20 to 25 minutes, or until edges are lightly browned. Cool completely. Sprinkle with powdered sugar. Cut into bars.

Makes about 3 dozen bars

ROCKY ROAD FUDGE BROWNIES

A rocky road topping of butterscotch, marshmallows and peanuts makes these fudge brownies super!

Bars
½ cup LAND O LAKES® Butter
2 squares (1 ounce each) unsweetened chocolate
2 eggs
1 cup sugar
⅔ cup all-purpose flour
¼ teaspoon salt
1 teaspoon vanilla

Topping
½ cup chopped salted peanuts
½ cup butterscotch chips
1 cup miniature marshmallows
¼ cup chocolate ice cream topping

Heat oven to 350°. For bars, in heavy, small saucepan, combine butter and chocolate. Cook, stirring constantly, over medium heat, until melted, 3 to 5 minutes; set aside.

In small mixer bowl, beat eggs at medium speed until light and fluffy, 2 to 3 minutes. Gradually beat in cooled chocolate mixture, sugar, flour, salt and vanilla, scraping bowl often, until well mixed, 1 to 2 minutes. Spread into greased 9-inch square baking pan. Bake for 20 to 25 minutes, or until brownies begin to pull away from sides of pan.

For topping, sprinkle nuts, butterscotch chips and marshmallows over hot brownies. Drizzle with ice cream topping. Continue baking for 12 to 18 minutes, or until lightly browned. Cool completely. Cut into bars.

Makes about 2 dozen bars

Irresistible Bars

This chapter has bars for everyone—buttery-rich shortbread, fruit, chocolate, nut and cheesecake. Most of these are so easy, you just mix, pat-in-the-pan and bake; then finish with glazes or wonderful-tasting fillings and toppings. Try them—they're sure to be a hit with your family and friends.

Pictured here are: Crisp 'n' Crunchy Almond Coconut Bars, page 36, and Strawberry Wonders, page 39.

CHERRY DATE SPARKLE BARS

This sinfully rich filling of dates, cherries and pecans tops a pie-like crust for an irresistible bar.

Crust
- 1 cup all-purpose flour
- ¼ cup sugar
- ½ cup LAND O LAKES® Butter, softened

Filling
- ¾ cup sugar
- ½ cup all-purpose flour
- 2 eggs
- ½ teaspoon baking powder
- ¼ teaspoon salt
- 1½ teaspoons vanilla
- ¾ cup chopped dates
- ½ cup flaked coconut
- ½ cup chopped pecans
- ½ cup halved maraschino cherries, drained

Heat oven to 350°. For crust, in small mixer bowl, combine all crust ingredients. Beat at low speed, scraping bowl often, until mixture is crumbly, 1 to 2 minutes. Press on bottom of ungreased 9-inch square baking pan. Bake for 15 to 20 minutes, or until edges are lightly browned.

For filling, in same mixer bowl, combine sugar, flour, eggs, baking powder, salt and vanilla. Beat at medium speed, scraping bowl often, until well mixed, 1 to 2 minutes. Stir in remaining ingredients. Pour over hot crust. Continue baking for 25 to 30 minutes, or until lightly browned and filling is set. Cool completely. Cut into bars.   *Makes about 3 dozen bars*

CRISP 'N' CRUNCHY ALMOND COCONUT BARS

Rum flavor adds a distinct difference from top to bottom in this two layer coconut almond bar.

Crust
- 1¼ cups all-purpose flour
- ¼ cup granulated sugar
- ½ cup LAND O LAKES® Butter, softened
- ½ teaspoon rum extract
- ¼ cup sliced almonds, toasted

Filling
- 1 cup powdered sugar
- ¼ cup LAND O LAKES® Butter
- ¼ cup milk
- 2 tablespoons all-purpose flour
- ½ teaspoon rum extract
- 1 cup flaked coconut
- 1 cup sliced almonds

Heat oven to 375°. For crust, in small mixer bowl, combine flour, granulated sugar, butter and rum extract. Beat at low speed, scraping bowl often, until mixture is crumbly, 1 to 2 minutes. Stir in nuts. Press on bottom of ungreased 9-inch square baking pan. Bake for 12 to 18 minutes, or until edges are lightly browned.

For filling, in small saucepan, combine powdered sugar, butter, milk, flour and rum extract. Cook, stirring constantly, over medium heat until mixture comes to a full boil, 5 to 7 minutes. Stir in coconut and almonds. Pour over crust. Continue baking for 11 to 16 minutes, or until lightly browned. Cool completely. Cut into bars.   *Makes about 2 dozen bars*

Cherry Date Sparkle Bars

Twist O'Lemon Cheesecakes

TWIST O'LEMON CHEESECAKES

The tang of lemon and the richness of cheesecake are combined in this buttery crusted bar.

Crust
- 2 cups all-purpose flour
- 1/2 cup sugar
- 3/4 cup LAND O LAKES® Butter, softened
- 1 tablespoon grated lemon peel

Filling
- 1 1/3 cups sugar
- 1/4 cup all-purpose flour
- 2 packages (3 ounces each) cream cheese, softened
- 4 eggs
- 1/4 cup lemon juice
- 1 teaspoon baking powder
- 1/2 teaspoon salt
- 1 tablespoon grated lemon peel
- 1 teaspoon vanilla
- 1 cup sliced almonds
- 1 teaspoon ground nutmeg

Heat oven to 350°. For crust, in large mixer bowl, combine all crust ingredients. Beat at low speed, scraping bowl often, until particles are fine, 1 to 2 minutes. Press on bottom of ungreased 13×9×2-inch baking pan. Bake for 15 to 20 minutes, or until edges are lightly browned.

For filling, in same mixer bowl, combine sugar, flour, cream cheese, eggs, lemon juice, baking powder, salt, lemon peel and vanilla. Beat at low speed, scraping bowl often, until well mixed, 1 to 2 minutes. Stir in almonds. Pour over hot crust. Continue baking for 20 to 25 minutes, or until knife inserted in center comes out clean. Sprinkle nutmeg over top. Cool completely. Cut into bars. Store, covered, in refrigerator.   *Makes about 3 dozen bars*

STRAWBERRY WONDERS

Come-for-coffee cookie bars that are buttery good and strawberry-filled.

Crust
- 1 1/2 cups all-purpose flour
- 1/2 cup quick-cooking oats
- 1/2 cup granulated sugar
- 3/4 cup LAND O LAKES® Butter, softened
- 1/2 teaspoon baking soda

Topping
- 3/4 cup flaked coconut
- 3/4 cup chopped walnuts
- 1/4 cup all-purpose flour
- 1/4 cup firmly packed brown sugar
- 2 tablespoons LAND O LAKES® Butter, softened
- 1/2 teaspoon ground cinnamon
- 1 jar (10 ounces) strawberry preserves

Heat oven to 350°. For crust, in large mixer bowl, combine all crust ingredients. Beat at low speed, scraping bowl often, until mixture is crumbly, 1 to 2 minutes. Press crust mixture on bottom of greased 13×9×2-inch baking pan. Bake for 18 to 22 minutes, or until edges are lightly browned.

For topping, in same mixer bowl, combine coconut, nuts, flour, brown sugar, butter and cinnamon. Beat at low speed, scraping bowl often, until well mixed, 1 to 2 minutes. Spread preserves to 1/4 inch of edges of hot crust. Sprinkle topping mixture over preserves. Continue baking for 18 to 22 minutes, or until edges are lightly browned. Cool completely. Cut into bars.   *Makes about 3 dozen bars*

APPLE PIE BARS

Apple pie takes on a new look in these rich apple bars that are topped with a vanilla glaze.

Crust
    Milk
    1 egg yolk, reserve egg white
2½ cups all-purpose flour
    1 teaspoon salt
    1 cup LAND O LAKES® Butter,
        softened

Filling
    1 cup crushed corn flake cereal
    8 cups peeled, cored, ¼-inch
        sliced, tart cooking apples
        (about 8 to 10 medium)
    1 cup granulated sugar
1½ teaspoons ground cinnamon
    ½ teaspoon ground nutmeg
    1 reserved egg white
    2 tablespoons granulated sugar
    ½ teaspoon ground cinnamon

Glaze
    1 cup powdered sugar
    1 to 2 tablespoons milk
    ½ teaspoon vanilla

Heat oven to 350°. For crust, add enough milk to egg yolk to measure ⅔ cup; set aside. In medium bowl, combine flour and salt. Cut in butter until crumbly. With fork, stir in milk mixture until dough forms a ball; divide into halves. Roll out ½ of the dough, on lightly floured surface, into a 15×10-inch rectangle. Place on bottom of ungreased 15×10×1-inch jelly-roll pan.

For filling, sprinkle cereal over top; layer apples over cereal. In small bowl, combine 1 cup granulated sugar, 1½ teaspoons cinnamon and nutmeg. Sprinkle over apples. Roll remaining ½ of dough into a 15½×10½-inch rectangle; place over apples. In small bowl, with fork beat egg white until foamy; brush over top crust. In another small bowl, stir together 2 tablespoons granulated sugar and ½ teaspoon cinnamon; sprinkle over crust. Bake for 45 to 60 minutes, or until lightly browned.

For glaze, in small bowl, stir together all glaze ingredients. Drizzle over warm bars. Cut into bars. *Makes about 3 dozen bars*

Apple Pie Bars

Caramel Chocolate Pecan Bars

CARAMEL CHOCOLATE PECAN BARS

Caramel and chocolate top a buttery crumb crust—absolutely delicious!

Crust
- 2 cups all-purpose flour
- 1 cup firmly packed brown sugar
- ½ cup LAND O LAKES® Butter, softened
- 1 cup pecan halves

Filling
- ½ cup firmly packed brown sugar
- ⅔ cup LAND O LAKES® Butter
- ½ cup semi-sweet chocolate chips
- ½ cup butterscotch chips

Heat oven to 350°. For crust, in large mixer bowl, combine flour, sugar and butter. Beat at medium speed, scraping bowl often, until particles are fine, 2 to 3 minutes. Press on bottom of ungreased 13×9×2-inch baking pan. Sprinkle nuts over crust.

For filling, in small saucepan, combine sugar and butter. Cook, stirring constantly, over medium heat until mixture comes to a full boil, 4 to 5 minutes. Boil, stirring constantly, until candy thermometer reaches 242°F, or small amount of mixture dropped into ice water forms a firm ball, about 1 minute. Pour over pecans and crust.

Bake for 18 to 20 minutes, or until entire caramel layer is bubbly. Immediately sprinkle with chocolate and butterscotch chips. Let stand 3 to 5 minutes to melt chips. Swirl chips with tip of knife, leaving some whole for a marbled effect. Cool completely. Cut into bars.

Makes about 3 dozen bars

COCONUT DATE CANDY SQUARES

This easy confection is cooked on the range and then chilled in your refrigerator for a quick coconut date candy.

Bars
- 1 cup chopped dates
- ¾ cup granulated sugar
- ½ cup all-purpose flour
- ½ cup LAND O LAKES® Butter
- 1 egg
- 1½ cups flaked coconut

Glaze
- ¼ cup powdered sugar
- 2 teaspoons milk
- ½ teaspoon lemon juice
- ¼ teaspoon vanilla

For bars, in heavy, medium saucepan, combine dates, granulated sugar, flour, butter and egg. Cook, stirring constantly, over medium heat until mixture comes to a full boil, 7 to 9 minutes. Continue cooking, stirring constantly, until thickened, 3 minutes. Stir in coconut. Spread in greased 9×5×3-inch loaf pan.

For glaze, in small bowl, stir together all glaze ingredients. Drizzle glaze over warm bars. Cover; refrigerate until firm, about 3 hours. Cut into squares. Store, covered, in refrigerator.

Makes about 2 dozen squares

ALMOND MACAROON BARS

This rich macaroon bar is glorified with coconut and almonds.

Crust
1¾ cups all-purpose flour
½ cup sugar
¾ cup LAND O LAKES® Butter, softened
½ teaspoon ground nutmeg

Filling
1 cup sugar
2 eggs
2 tablespoons all-purpose flour
1 teaspoon baking powder
½ teaspoon salt
2 teaspoons vanilla
1 cup flaked coconut
1 cup toasted slivered almonds

Heat oven to 350°. For crust, in small mixer bowl, combine all crust ingredients. Beat at low speed, scraping bowl often, until particles are fine, 2 to 3 minutes. Press on bottom of ungreased 13×9×2-inch baking pan. Bake for 15 to 20 minutes, or until edges are lightly browned.

For filling, in same mixer bowl, combine sugar, eggs, flour, baking powder, salt and vanilla. Beat at medium speed, scraping bowl often, until well mixed, 1 to 2 minutes. Stir in coconut and almonds. Pour filling over hot crust. Continue baking for 15 to 20 minutes, or until lightly browned. Cool completely. Cut into bars.   *Makes about 3 dozen bars*

SPICE 'N' EASY
APPLE RAISIN BARS

These buttery good homemade bars are quick to make and full of flavor.

Crumb Mixture
2 cups all-purpose flour
2 cups quick-cooking oats
1½ cups sugar
1¼ cups LAND O LAKES® Butter, melted
1 teaspoon baking soda

Filling
½ cup raisins
½ cup chopped pecans
1 can (20 ounces) apple fruit filling
½ teaspoon ground cinnamon
½ teaspoon ground nutmeg

Heat oven to 350°. For crumb mixture, in large bowl, combine all crumb ingredients. Stir until well mixed, 1 to 2 minutes. Reserve 1½ cups of the crumb mixture. Press remaining crumb mixture on bottom of ungreased 13×9×2-inch baking pan. Bake for 15 to 20 minutes, or until edges are lightly browned.

For filling, in same bowl, combine all filling ingredients. Stir to blend. Spread over hot crust. Sprinkle 1½ cups reserved crumb mixture over top. Continue baking for 25 to 30 minutes, or until lightly browned. Cool completely. Cut into bars.   *Makes about 3 dozen bars*

Almond Macaroon Bars

Frosted Honey Bars

FROSTED HONEY BARS

Carrots and honey make these bars extra moist. Cream cheese frosting is the finishing touch.

Bars
1½ cups all-purpose flour
1 cup LAND O LAKES® Butter, melted
1 cup honey
3 eggs
1½ teaspoons baking soda
1 teaspoon ground cinnamon
¾ teaspoon salt
1½ cups shredded carrots (about 3 medium)
¾ cup chopped walnuts

Frosting
1 cup powdered sugar
1 package (8 ounces) cream cheese, softened
1 teaspoon milk
1 teaspoon vanilla

Heat oven to 350°. For bars, in large mixer bowl, combine flour, butter, honey, eggs, baking soda, cinnamon and salt. Beat at low speed, scraping bowl often, until well mixed, 1 to 2 minutes. Stir in carrots and nuts. Pour into greased 15×10×1-inch jelly-roll pan. Bake for 20 to 25 minutes, or until top springs back when touched lightly in center. Cool completely.

For frosting, in small mixer bowl, combine all frosting ingredients. Beat at medium speed, scraping bowl often, until smooth, 1 to 2 minutes. Spread bars with frosting. Cut into bars. Store, covered, in refrigerator.

Makes about 3 dozen bars

SUNNY LEMON OATMEAL BARS

The ultimate in tenderness is found inside this lemon oatmeal bar.

Bars
1¼ cups all-purpose flour
¾ cup quick-cooking oats
⅔ cup granulated sugar
1 cup LAND O LAKES® Butter, softened
½ cup milk
1 egg
1 teaspoon baking soda
½ teaspoon salt
1 tablespoon grated lemon peel
1 teaspoon vanilla

Glaze
1 cup powdered sugar
2 tablespoons lemon juice
1 tablespoon grated lemon peel

Heat oven to 375°. For bars, in large mixer bowl, combine all bar ingredients. Beat at low speed, scraping bowl often, until well mixed, 1 to 2 minutes. Spread into ungreased 13×9×2-inch baking pan. Bake for 15 to 20 minutes, or until wooden pick inserted in center comes out clean.

For glaze, in small bowl, combine all glaze ingredients; stir until smooth. Spread over warm bars. Cool completely. Cut into bars.

Makes about 3 dozen bars

JAN HAGEL

This traditional Scandinavian bar just melts in your mouth.

---

2 cups all-purpose flour
1 cup sugar
1 cup LAND O LAKES® Butter,
   softened

1 egg, separated
1 teaspoon ground cinnamon
½ teaspoon salt
1 cup sliced almonds

Heat oven to 350°. In large mixer bowl, combine flour, sugar, butter, egg yolk, cinnamon and salt. Beat at low speed, scraping bowl often, until well mixed, 2 to 3 minutes. Divide dough into halves. Press each half onto an ungreased cookie sheet to 1/16-inch thickness. In small bowl, beat egg white with fork until foamy. Brush over dough; sprinkle with nuts. Bake for 12 to 15 minutes, or until very lightly browned. Immediately cut into 2-inch squares and remove from pan. Cool completely.

Makes 3 to 4 dozen squares

ORANGE DATE TREASURE BARS

Help yourself to this luxuriously moist, old-fashioned date bar.

Bars
  1 package (8 ounces) chopped
    dates
 ¾ cup granulated sugar
 ½ cup LAND O LAKES® Butter
 ½ cup water
1¼ cups all-purpose flour
  1 cup chopped pecans
 ¾ cup milk
 ¼ cup orange juice
  2 eggs

¾ teaspoon baking soda
¼ teaspoon salt
1 tablespoon grated orange peel

Frosting
3 cups powdered sugar
⅓ cup LAND O LAKES® Butter,
   softened
3 tablespoons milk
1 tablespoon grated orange peel

Heat oven to 350°. For bars, in large saucepan, combine dates, granulated sugar, butter and water. Cook, stirring constantly, over low heat, until dates are softened, 5 to 8 minutes. Remove from heat; stir in flour, nuts, milk, orange juice, eggs, baking soda, salt and orange peel. Spread onto greased 15×10×1-inch jelly-roll pan. Bake for 15 to 20 minutes, or until wooden pick inserted in center comes out clean. Cool completely.

For frosting, in small bowl, combine all frosting ingredients. Beat at medium speed, scraping bowl often, until light and fluffy, 1 to 2 minutes. Spread over bars. Cut into bars. *Makes about 4 dozen bars*

Jan Hagel

Citrus Pie Bars

CITRUS PIE BARS

These moist pie-like bars have just the right touch of tropical flavor.

Crust
- 1 cup all-purpose flour
- ¼ cup sugar
- ⅓ cup LAND O LAKES® Butter, softened
- ¼ teaspoon ground cardamom or mace

Filling
- ½ cup sugar
- ½ cup flaked coconut
- 2 eggs
- 2 tablespoons all-purpose flour
- ½ teaspoon baking powder
- ⅛ teaspoon salt
- 2 tablespoons grated lemon or orange peel
- 2 tablespoons lemon juice

Heat oven to 350°. For crust, in small mixer bowl, combine all crust ingredients. Beat at low speed, scraping bowl often, until particles are fine, 1 to 2 minutes. Press on bottom of ungreased 8-inch square baking pan. Bake for 12 to 17 minutes, or until edges are lightly browned.

For filling, in same mixer bowl, combine all filling ingredients. Beat at medium speed, scraping bowl often, until well mixed, 1 to 2 minutes. Pour over hot crust. Continue baking for 15 to 20 minutes, or until edges are lightly brown. Cool completely. Cut into bars.

Makes about 2 dozen bars

PINEAPPLE CHEESECAKE BARS

Cheesecake bars made special with candied pineapple.

Crumb Mixture
- 1¼ cups all-purpose flour
- ⅓ cup sugar
- ½ cup LAND O LAKES® Butter
- 1 tablespoon grated orange peel

Filling
- 1 package (8 ounces) cream cheese, softened
- ¼ cup sugar
- 1 egg
- 1 tablespoon lemon juice
- ½ cup chopped candied pineapple

Heat oven to 350°. For crumb mixture, in small mixer bowl, combine all crumb mixture ingredients. Beat at low speed, scraping bowl often, until well mixed, 1 to 2 minutes. Reserve ½ cup of the crumb mixture. Press remaining crumb mixture on bottom of ungreased 8-inch square baking pan. Bake for 12 to 17 minutes, or until edges are lightly browned.

For filling, in same mixer bowl, combine cream cheese, sugar, egg and lemon juice. Beat at medium speed, scraping bowl often, until mixture is light and fluffy, 1 to 2 minutes. Stir in pineapple. Spread filling over hot crust. Sprinkle ½ cup reserved crumb mixture over top. Continue baking for 15 to 20 minutes, or until edges are lightly browned. Cool completely. Cut into bars. Store, covered, in refrigerator.

Makes about 2 dozen bars

GLAZED RUM RAISIN BARS

The pleasing flavor combination of rum and raisin team up in this moist bar topped with a buttery rum glaze.

Bars
½ cup water
1 cup raisins
2 cups all-purpose flour
¾ cup granulated sugar
1 cup LAND O LAKES® Butter,
   softened
½ cup milk
1 egg
1 teaspoon baking powder

1 teaspoon salt
½ teaspoon rum extract

Glaze
¼ cup LAND O LAKES® Butter
¾ cup powdered sugar
1 tablespoon water
¼ teaspoon rum extract

Heat oven to 375°. For bars, in heavy, small saucepan, combine water and raisins. Cook over medium heat until water comes to a full boil, 3 to 4 minutes. Drain water; reserve raisins.

In large mixer bowl, combine flour, granulated sugar, butter, milk, egg, baking powder, salt and rum extract. Beat at low speed, scraping bowl often, until well mixed, 2 to 3 minutes. Stir in drained raisins. Spread into ungreased 13×9×2-inch baking pan. Bake for 20 to 25 minutes, or until wooden pick inserted in center comes out clean.

For glaze, in same saucepan, melt butter over low heat, 3 to 4 minutes. Add powdered sugar, water and rum extract. Cook, stirring occasionally, until smooth, 1 to 2 minutes. Spread glaze over warm bars. Cool completely. Cut into bars. *Makes about 3 dozen bars*

HONEY NUT CHESS BARS

These bars are rich with butter, honey and nuts and will be as well liked as chess pie.

Crust
1¼ cups all-purpose flour
⅓ cup granulated sugar
½ cup LAND O LAKES® Butter,
   softened
¼ cup chopped pecans

Filling
1 cup firmly packed brown sugar
½ cup chopped pecans
½ cup LAND O LAKES® Butter,
   melted
2 eggs
2 tablespoons honey

Heat oven to 350°. For crust, in small mixer bowl, combine flour, sugar and butter. Beat at low speed, scraping bowl often, until mixture is crumbly, 1 to 2 minutes. Stir in nuts. Press on bottom of ungreased 9-inch square baking pan. Bake for 15 to 20 minutes, or until edges are lightly browned.

For filling, in same mixer bowl, combine all filling ingredients. Beat at low speed, scraping bowl often, until well mixed, 1 to 2 minutes. Pour over hot crust. Continue baking for 25 to 30 minutes, or until wooden pick inserted in center comes out clean. Cool completely. Cut into bars. *Makes about 3 dozen bars*

Glazed Rum Raisin Bars; Pineapple
Cheesecake Bars, page 51

The Family Collection

Cookies make great treats for the whole family—easy to pack for coffee breaks, school lunches or outings. What could be better than to surprise your family with Old-Fashioned Butter Cookies, Chocolate Pixies or Spiced Molasses Cookies!

Pictured here are: Fruit Filled Thumbprints, page 56; Lemon Meltaways, page 56; and Peanut Buttery Cookies, page 57.

LEMON MELTAWAYS

These tiny refrigerator cookies are lemon flavored with lemon frosting.

Cookies
1¼ cups all-purpose flour
½ cup cornstarch
⅓ cup powdered sugar
¾ cup LAND O LAKES® Butter,
    softened
1 tablespoon lemon juice
1 teaspoon lemon peel

Frosting
¾ cup powdered sugar
¼ cup LAND O LAKES® Butter,
    softened
1 teaspoon lemon juice
1 teaspoon grated lemon peel

For cookies, in large mixer bowl, combine all cookie ingredients. Beat at low speed, scraping bowl often, until well mixed, 2 to 3 minutes. Shape dough into two 8×1-inch rolls. Wrap in waxed paper. Refrigerate until firm, 1 to 2 hours.

Heat oven to 350°. Cut rolls into ¼-inch slices. Place 2 inches apart on ungreased cookie sheets. Bake for 8 to 12 minutes, or until set; cookies will not brown. Remove immediately; cool completely.

For frosting, in small mixer bowl, combine all frosting ingredients. Beat at medium speed, scraping bowl often, until light and fluffy, 1 to 2 minutes. Spread on cooled cookies. *Makes about 4 dozen cookies*

FRUIT FILLED THUMBPRINTS

These tender butter cookies are rolled in nuts and filled with fruit preserves.

2 cups all-purpose flour
½ cup firmly packed brown sugar
1 cup LAND O LAKES® Butter,
    softened
2 eggs, separated

⅛ teaspoon salt
1 teaspoon vanilla
1½ cups finely chopped pecans
    Fruit preserves

Heat oven to 350°. In large mixer bowl, combine flour, sugar, butter, egg yolks, salt and vanilla. Beat at low speed, scraping bowl often, until well mixed, 2 to 3 minutes. Shape rounded teaspoonfuls of dough into 1-inch balls. In small bowl, beat egg whites with fork until foamy. Dip each ball into whites; roll in nuts. Place 1 inch apart on greased cookie sheets. Make a depression in center of each cookie with back of teaspoon. Bake for 8 minutes; remove from oven. Fill centers with preserves. Continue baking for 6 to 10 minutes, or until lightly browned.

Makes about 3 dozen cookies

PEANUT BUTTERY COOKIES

These buttery cookies are chock-full of peanuts for extra flavor and crunch.

1½ cups all-purpose flour
½ cup granulated sugar
½ cup firmly packed brown sugar
½ cup LAND O LAKES® Butter, softened
2 eggs

1 teaspoon salt
½ teaspoon baking soda
½ teaspoon vanilla
2 cups salted peanuts (about 12 ounces)

Heat oven to 350°. In large mixer bowl, combine flour, granulated sugar, brown sugar, butter, eggs, salt, baking soda and vanilla. Beat at low speed, scraping bowl often, until well mixed, 2 to 3 minutes. Stir in nuts. Drop rounded teaspoonfuls of dough 2 inches apart onto greased cookie sheets. Bake for 8 to 12 minutes, or until lightly browned. Remove immediately.

Makes about 4 dozen cookies

COUNTRY SOUR CREAM COOKIES

Passed on to three generations of moms, these cutout cookies are a holiday favorite.

4 cups all-purpose flour
2 cups sugar
1 cup LAND O LAKES® Butter, softened
½ cup dairy sour cream
2 eggs
1 tablespoon baking powder

1 teaspoon baking soda
½ teaspoon salt
½ teaspoon ground nutmeg
1 teaspoon vanilla
½ teaspoon lemon extract
Sugar for sprinkling

In large mixer bowl, combine 2 cups of the flour, 2 cups sugar, butter, sour cream, eggs, baking powder, baking soda, salt, nutmeg, vanilla and lemon extract. Beat at low speed, scraping bowl often, until well mixed, 2 to 3 minutes. Stir in remaining 2 cups flour. Divide dough into 4 equal portions. Wrap in waxed paper. Refrigerate until firm, at least 2 hours.

Heat oven to 350°. Roll out dough on well-floured surface to ⅛-inch thickness. Cut out with cookie cutters. Place 1 inch apart on ungreased cookie sheets. Sprinkle sugar over tops. Bake for 8 to 12 minutes, or until edges are lightly browned.

Makes about 6 dozen cookies

Note: Dough may be tinted with a few drops of food coloring, before it is refrigerated.

BANANA CREAM SANDWICH COOKIES

These banana cookies are fun to make and are filled with a buttery frosting for a delicious sandwich cookie.

Cookies
2⅓ cups all-purpose flour
1 cup granulated sugar
1 cup LAND O LAKES® Butter, softened
½ cup banana cut into ¼-inch slices (about 1 medium)
¼ teaspoon salt
1 teaspoon vanilla
½ cup chopped pecans

Frosting
3 cups powdered sugar
⅓ cup LAND O LAKES® Butter, softened
3 to 4 tablespoons milk
1 teaspoon vanilla
Food coloring (optional)

Heat oven to 350°. For cookies, in large mixer bowl, combine flour, granulated sugar, butter, banana, salt and vanilla. Beat at low speed, scraping bowl often, until well mixed, 2 to 3 minutes. Stir in nuts. Shape rounded teaspoonfuls of dough into 1-inch balls. Place 2 inches apart on greased cookie sheets. Flatten cookie to ¼-inch thickness with bottom of glass dipped in flour. Bake for 12 to 15 minutes, or until edges are lightly browned. Remove immediately; cool completely.

For frosting, in small mixer bowl, combine all frosting ingredients. Beat at medium speed, scraping bowl often, until light and fluffy, 1 to 2 minutes. If desired, tint with food coloring. Spread 1 tablespoon of frosting over bottoms of ½ of the cookies. Top with remaining cookies.

Makes about 2 dozen sandwich cookies

OLD-FASHIONED BUTTER COOKIES

Passed down for four generations, this buttery sugar cookie recipe brings back fond memories of Grandma's cookie jar.

¾ cup sugar
1 cup LAND O LAKES® Butter, softened
2 egg yolks

1 teaspoon vanilla
2 cups all-purpose flour
¼ teaspoon salt
Pecan halves

Heat oven to 350°. In large mixer bowl, combine sugar, butter, egg yolks and vanilla. Beat at medium speed, scraping bowl often, until well mixed, 1 to 2 minutes. Add flour and salt; beat at low speed, scraping bowl often, until well mixed, 2 to 3 minutes. Shape rounded teaspoonfuls of dough into 1-inch balls. Place 2 inches apart on ungreased cookie sheets. Flatten cookie to ¼-inch thickness with bottom of glass dipped in sugar. Place pecan half in center of each cookie. Bake for 10 to 12 minutes, or until edges are lightly browned. Cool 1 minute; remove from cookie sheets.

Makes about 2½ dozen cookies

Banana Cream Sandwich Cookies

FAVORITE BUTTER COOKIES

These crisp, tender cutout cookies can be decorated to capture the spirit of your occasion.

Cookies
2½ cups all-purpose flour
1 cup granulated sugar
1 cup LAND O LAKES® Butter,
   softened
1 egg
1 teaspoon baking powder
2 tablespoons orange juice
1 tablespoon vanilla

Frosting
4 cups powdered sugar
½ cup LAND O LAKES® Butter,
   softened
3 to 4 tablespoons milk
2 teaspoons vanilla
   Food coloring, colored sugars,
   flaked coconut and
   cinnamon candies for
   decorations

For cookies, in large mixer bowl, combine all cookie ingredients. Beat at low speed, scraping bowl often, until well mixed, 1 to 2 minutes. If desired, divide dough into 3 equal portions; color ⅔ of the dough with desired food colorings. Mix until dough is evenly colored. Wrap in waxed paper. Refrigerate until firm, 2 to 3 hours.

Heat oven to 400°. Roll out dough, ⅓ at a time, on well-floured surface to ¼-inch thickness. Cut out with cookie cutters. Place 1 inch apart on ungreased cookie sheets. If desired, sprinkle colored sugars over tops, or bake and decorate later. Bake for 6 to 10 minutes, or until edges are lightly browned. Remove immediately; cool completely.

For frosting, in small mixer bowl, combine powdered sugar, butter, milk and vanilla. Beat at low speed, scraping bowl often, until fluffy, 1 to 2 minutes. Frost or decorate cooled cookies.

Makes about 3 dozen cookies

Decorating ideas:
Wreaths: Cut out cookies with 2-inch round cookie cutter; bake as directed. Frost with green colored frosting. Color coconut green; sprinkle frosted cookies with coconut. Place 3 cinnamon candies together to resemble holly.

Christmas trees: Color dough green; cut out with Christmas tree cutter. Sprinkle with colored sugars; bake as directed.

Angels: Cut out cookies with angel cookie cutter; bake as directed. Use blue frosting for dress, yellow frosting for hair and white frosting for wings, face and lace on dress.

Candy and Peanut Jumbles

CANDY AND PEANUT JUMBLES

You'll receive lots of requests for these colorful cookies.

1 cup granulated sugar	1½ cups quick-cooking oats
1 cup firmly packed brown sugar	1 teaspoon baking soda
1 cup LAND O LAKES® Butter, softened	½ teaspoon salt
2 eggs	2 cups (1 pound) candy coated milk chocolate pieces
1 tablespoon vanilla	1 cup coarsely chopped salted peanuts
2 cups all-purpose flour	

Heat oven to 350°. In large mixer bowl, combine granulated sugar, brown sugar, butter, eggs and vanilla. Beat at medium speed, scraping bowl often, until light and fluffy, 2 to 3 minutes. Add flour, oats, baking soda and salt. Beat at medium speed, scraping bowl often, until well mixed, 2 to 3 minutes. Stir in candy and nuts. Drop scant ¼ cupfuls of dough 2 inches apart onto greased cookie sheets. Bake for 14 to 18 minutes, or until golden brown. Remove immediately. *Makes about 2 dozen cookies*

HONEY 'N' SPICE COOKIES

Orange, honey, nutmeg and cloves team up in these buttery tender, soft drop cookies.

Cookies	½ teaspoon ground nutmeg
2 cups all-purpose flour	¼ teaspoon ground cloves
¾ cup granulated sugar	½ teaspoon orange extract or vanilla
¾ cup LAND O LAKES® Butter, softened	
¼ cup honey	**Glaze**
1 egg	1 cup powdered sugar
½ teaspoon salt	2 tablespoons milk
½ teaspoon baking soda	2 teaspoons grated orange peel

Heat oven to 375°. For cookies, in large mixer bowl, combine all cookie ingredients. Beat at low speed, scraping bowl often, until well mixed, 1 to 2 minutes. Drop rounded teaspoonfuls of dough 2 inches apart onto ungreased cookie sheets. Bake for 7 to 10 minutes, or until edges are lightly browned. Remove immediately.

For glaze, in small bowl, stir together all glaze ingredients. Frost warm cookies with glaze. *Makes about 3 dozen cookies*

MAPLE RAISIN COOKIES

These maple-flavored cookies also include applesauce for a moist country-fresh cookie.

Cookies
2¼ cups all-purpose flour
1 cup granulated sugar
¾ cup LAND O LAKES® Butter,
    softened
¾ cup applesauce
1 egg
1 teaspoon pumpkin pie spice
½ teaspoon baking soda
½ teaspoon salt

1 cup raisins
½ cup chopped walnuts

Frosting
4 cups powdered sugar
½ cup LAND O LAKES® Butter,
    softened
3 to 4 tablespoons milk
½ teaspoon maple extract
Raisins

Heat oven to 375°. For cookies, in large mixer bowl, combine flour, granulated sugar, butter, applesauce, egg, pumpkin pie spice, baking soda and salt. Beat at low speed, scraping bowl often, until well mixed, 2 to 3 minutes. Stir in raisins and nuts. Drop rounded teaspoonfuls of dough 2 inches apart onto greased cookie sheets. Bake for 10 to 12 minutes, or until lightly browned. Remove immediately; cool completely.

For frosting, in small mixer bowl, combine powdered sugar, butter, milk and maple extract. Beat at medium speed, scraping bowl often, until light and fluffy, 3 to 4 minutes. Spread over cooled cookies. Place 2 raisins in center of each cookie. *Makes about 3 dozen cookies*

CORNISH BISCUIT COOKIES

These soft cookies, filled with raisins, have been a traditional family recipe for over 100 years.

3½ cups all-purpose flour
¾ cup firmly packed brown sugar
½ cup granulated sugar
1 cup LAND O LAKES® Butter,
    softened
1 cup milk
2 eggs

2 teaspoons baking powder
½ teaspoon baking soda
½ teaspoon salt
2 teaspoons vanilla
1 cup raisins
Granulated sugar for
    sprinkling

Heat oven to 375°. In large mixer bowl, combine flour, brown sugar, granulated sugar, butter, milk, eggs, baking powder, baking soda, salt and vanilla. Beat at low speed, scraping bowl often, until well mixed, 2 to 3 minutes. Stir in raisins. Drop rounded teaspoonfuls of dough 2 inches apart onto greased cookie sheets. Sprinkle sugar over tops. Bake for 8 to 10 minutes, or until edges are lightly browned. Remove immediately.

Makes about 7 dozen cookies

Maple Raisin Cookies

Honey of a Cookie; Spiced Molasses
Cookies

HONEY OF A COOKIE

These golden cookies blend popular flavors of honey and carrot into a moist, chewy cookie.

2½ cups all-purpose flour
1 cup sugar
⅔ cup LAND O LAKES® Butter
2 eggs
¼ cup honey
2 teaspoons baking powder

½ teaspoon pumpkin pie spice
¼ teaspoon salt
1 teaspoon vanilla
½ cup shredded carrot (about 1 medium)

Heat oven to 325°. In large mixer bowl, combine flour, sugar, butter, eggs, honey, baking powder, pumpkin pie spice, salt and vanilla. Beat at low speed, scraping bowl often, until well mixed, 2 to 3 minutes. Stir in carrot. Shape rounded teaspoonfuls of dough into 1-inch balls. Place 2 inches apart on ungreased cookie sheets. Bake for 13 to 18 minutes, or until edges are lightly browned. Remove immediately.

Makes about 4 dozen cookies

SPICED MOLASSES COOKIES

The old-fashioned flavor of molasses is revived in these spicy, chewy cookies.

2¼ cups all-purpose flour
1 cup sugar
½ cup LAND O LAKES® Butter, softened
½ cup light molasses
¼ cup milk

1 egg
½ teaspoon baking soda
½ teaspoon ground ginger
¼ teaspoon ground cinnamon
⅛ teaspoon salt
Sugar for rolling

In large mixer bowl, combine flour, 1 cup sugar, butter, molasses, milk, egg, baking soda, ginger, cinnamon and salt. Beat at low speed, scraping bowl often, until well mixed, 2 to 3 minutes. Cover; refrigerate until firm, at least 2 hours.

Heat oven to 350°. Shape rounded teaspoonfuls of dough into 1-inch balls. Roll in sugar. Place 2 inches apart on ungreased cookie sheets. Bake for 10 to 12 minutes, or until slightly firm to the touch. Remove immediately.

Makes about 4½ dozen cookies

CHOCOLATE MERINGUE PEANUT SQUARES

These one-bake bars have a shortbread crust that is topped with a chocolate peanut meringue.

Crust
1½ cups all-purpose flour
½ cup sugar
¾ cup LAND O LAKES® Butter, softened
2 egg yolks, reserve egg whites
2 teaspoons vanilla

Filling
2 reserved egg whites
⅓ cup sugar
1 cup chopped salted peanuts
½ cup milk chocolate chips

Heat oven to 325°. For crust, in large mixer bowl, combine all crust ingredients. Beat at low speed, scraping bowl often, until mixture is crumbly, 1 to 2 minutes. Press onto bottom of greased 13×9×2-inch baking pan.

For filling, in small bowl, beat egg whites at high speed, scraping bowl often, until soft mounds form, 1 to 2 minutes. Gradually add sugar; beat until stiff peaks form, 1 to 2 minutes. Fold in peanuts and chocolate chips. Spread over crust. Bake for 30 to 35 minutes, or until lightly browned. Cool completely. Cut into squares. *Makes about 3 dozen squares*

BLACK WALNUT REFRIGERATOR COOKIES

Black walnuts bring a unique flavor to buttery sliced cookies.

3 cups all-purpose flour
1 cup firmly packed brown sugar
1 cup LAND O LAKES® Butter, softened
2 eggs

1 teaspoon baking soda
1 teaspoon cream of tartar
¼ teaspoon salt
1 teaspoon vanilla
1 cup chopped black walnuts

In large mixer bowl, combine flour, sugar, butter, eggs, baking soda, cream of tartar, salt and vanilla. Beat at low speed, scraping bowl often, until well mixed, 3 to 4 minutes. Stir in nuts. Divide dough into halves. Shape each half into a 12×2-inch roll. Wrap in waxed paper; refrigerate until firm, at least 2 hours.

Heat oven to 350°. Cut rolls into ¼-inch slices. Place 1 inch apart on ungreased cookie sheets. Bake for 9 to 12 minutes, or until lightly browned. Remove immediately. *Makes about 8 dozen cookies*

Chocolate Meringue Peanut Squares

Chocolate Pixies;
Lemon-Butter Snowbars

CHOCOLATE PIXIES

These chocolate cookies' powdered sugar-coating forms a unique crinkled design during baking.

¼ cup LAND O LAKES® Butter
4 squares (1 ounce each)
   unsweetened chocolate
2 cups all-purpose flour, divided
2 cups granulated sugar

4 eggs
2 teaspoons baking powder
½ teaspoon salt
½ cup chopped walnuts or pecans
   Powdered sugar for rolling

In small saucepan, melt butter and chocolate over low heat, 8 to 10 minutes. Cool. In large mixer bowl, combine melted chocolate mixture, 1 cup of the flour, granulated sugar, eggs, baking powder and salt. Beat at medium speed, scraping bowl often, until well mixed, 2 to 3 minutes. Stir in remaining 1 cup flour and the nuts. Cover; refrigerate until firm, at least 2 hours.

Heat oven to 300°. Shape rounded teaspoonfuls of dough into 1-inch balls; roll in powdered sugar. Place 2 inches apart on greased cookie sheets. Bake for 12 to 15 minutes, or until firm to the touch. Remove immediately.

Makes about 4 dozen cookies

LEMON-BUTTER SNOWBARS

These classic, buttery lemon bars are an all-time favorite.

Crust
1⅓ cups all-purpose flour
¼ cup granulated sugar
½ cup LAND O LAKES® Butter,
   softened

Filling
¾ cup granulated sugar
2 eggs
2 tablespoons all-purpose flour
¼ teaspoon baking powder
3 tablespoons lemon juice
   Powdered sugar for sprinkling

Heat oven to 350°. For crust, in small mixer bowl, combine all crust ingredients. Beat at low speed, scraping bowl often, until mixture is crumbly, 2 to 3 minutes. Press on bottom of ungreased 8-inch square baking pan. Bake for 15 to 20 minutes, or until edges are lightly browned.

For filling, in small mixer bowl, combine granulated sugar, eggs, flour, baking powder and lemon juice. Beat at low speed, scraping bowl often, until well mixed, 1 to 2 minutes. Pour over hot crust. Continue baking for 18 to 20 minutes, or until filling is set. Sprinkle with powdered sugar; cool completely. Cut into bars. *Makes 16 bars*

BUTTERY BUTTERSCOTCH CUTOUTS

This buttery cookie has melted butterscotch stirred in for that special flavor.

3 cups all-purpose flour
1 cup butterscotch chips, melted
½ cup granulated sugar
½ cup firmly packed brown sugar
1 cup LAND O LAKES® Butter, softened

1 egg
2 tablespoons milk
2 teaspoons vanilla
Powdered sugar for sprinkling

In large mixer bowl, combine flour, melted butterscotch chips, granulated sugar, brown sugar, butter, egg, milk and vanilla. Beat at low speed, scraping bowl often, until well mixed, 1 to 2 minutes. Divide dough into halves. Wrap in waxed paper; refrigerate until firm, 1 to 2 hours.

Heat oven to 375°. Roll out dough on well-floured surface to ⅛-inch thickness. Cut out with 2½-inch cookie cutter. Place 1 inch apart on ungreased cookie sheets. Bake for 5 to 8 minutes, or until edges are lightly browned. Remove immediately; cool completely. Sprinkle with powdered sugar or decorate as desired. *Makes about 4 dozen cookies*

CINNAMON RAISIN OATMEAL COOKIES

These old-fashioned raisin oatmeal spice cookies will be a cookie jar favorite.

3 cups quick-cooking oats
2 cups firmly packed brown sugar
1 cup LAND O LAKES® Butter, softened
2 eggs

1 teaspoon baking soda
1 teaspoon ground cinnamon
½ teaspoon salt
2 teaspoons vanilla
1½ cups all-purpose flour
1½ cups raisins

Heat oven to 375°. In large mixer bowl, combine oats, sugar, butter, eggs, baking soda, cinnamon, salt and vanilla. Beat at low speed, scraping bowl often, until well mixed, 1 to 2 minutes. Stir in flour until well mixed, 1 to 2 minutes. Stir in raisins. Drop rounded teaspoonfuls of dough 2 inches apart onto greased cookie sheets. Bake for 8 to 10 minutes, or until edges are lightly browned. Remove immediately. *Makes about 4 dozen cookies*

Buttery Butterscotch Cutouts

Lemon-Nut Cookies

LEMON-NUT COOKIES

A rich butter cookie that is lightly flavored with lemon and has the crunch of pecans.

2¾ cups all-purpose flour
1½ cups sugar
¾ cup LAND O LAKES® Butter,
    softened
2 eggs
1 teaspoon baking soda

½ teaspoon cream of tartar
½ teaspoon salt
2 tablespoons lemon juice
1 tablespoon grated lemon peel
2 teaspoons vanilla
1 cup chopped pecans

Heat oven to 400°. In large mixer bowl, combine flour, sugar, butter, eggs, baking soda, cream of tartar, salt, lemon juice, lemon peel and vanilla. Beat at low speed, scraping bowl often, until well mixed, 2 to 3 minutes. Stir in nuts. Shape rounded teaspoonfuls of dough into 1-inch balls. Place 2 inches apart on ungreased cookie sheets. Bake for 8 to 10 minutes, or until edges are lightly browned. Remove immediately.

Makes about 4 dozen cookies

SOUR CREAM
BROWN BUTTER COOKIES

Sour cream and brown butter frosting make these moist, tender cookies extra delicious.

Cookies
2⅓ cups all-purpose flour
1½ cups granulated sugar
½ cup LAND O LAKES® Butter,
    softened
2 eggs
1 teaspoon baking soda
½ teaspoon baking powder
½ teaspoon salt

2 teaspoons vanilla
½ cup chopped pecans
1 cup dairy sour cream

Frosting
½ cup LAND O LAKES® Butter
2 cups powdered sugar
2 to 3 tablespoons water
1 teaspoon vanilla

Heat oven to 350°. For cookies, in large mixer bowl, combine flour, granulated sugar, butter, eggs, baking soda, baking powder, salt and vanilla. Beat at low speed, scraping bowl often, until well mixed, 2 to 3 minutes. Stir in nuts and sour cream. Drop rounded teaspoonfuls of dough 2 inches apart onto greased cookie sheets. Bake for 8 to 12 minutes, or until edges are lightly browned. Remove immediately; cool completely.

For frosting, in heavy, small saucepan melt butter, stirring constantly, over low heat until butter is golden brown, 3 to 5 minutes. Stir in remaining ingredients until smooth. Spread over cooled cookies.

Makes about 5 dozen cookies

Extra-Special Cookies

Impress your family and friends with these stunning and scrumptious cookies. The collection in this chapter includes holiday favorites, elegant occasion specialties and heavenly rich cookies. All are perfect for entertaining.

Pictured here are: Lace Cookie Cups with Ice Cream, page 79, and Pecan Tartlets, page 80.

Almond Brickle Sugar Cookies

ALMOND BRICKLE SUGAR COOKIES

These tender butter cookies can be made two ways.

2¼ cups all-purpose flour
  1 cup sugar
  1 cup LAND O LAKES® Butter,
    softened
  1 egg

1 teaspoon baking soda
1 teaspoon vanilla
1 package (6 ounces) almond
  brickle bits*

Heat oven to 350°. In large mixer bowl, combine flour, sugar, butter, egg, baking soda and vanilla. Beat at medium speed, scraping bowl often, until well mixed, 2 to 3 minutes. Stir in almond brickle bits. Shape rounded teaspoonfuls of dough into 1-inch balls. Place 2 inches apart on greased cookie sheets. Flatten cookies to ¼-inch thickness with bottom of glass dipped in sugar. Bake for 8 to 11 minutes, or until edges are very lightly browned.

Makes about 4 dozen cookies

*You may substitute 1 cup mini semi-sweet chocolate chips for the almond brickle bits.

LACE COOKIE CUPS WITH ICE CREAM

Make cookie cups a day ahead. Just before serving, fill and drizzle with chocolate.

½ cup light corn syrup
½ cup LAND O LAKES® Butter
 1 cup all-purpose flour
½ cup firmly packed brown sugar
½ cup slivered almonds, finely
  chopped

Semi-sweet chocolate chips,
  melted*
Favorite ice cream

Heat oven to 300°. In medium saucepan, bring corn syrup to a full boil over medium heat, 2 to 3 minutes. Add butter; reduce heat to low. Cook, stirring occasionally, until butter melts, 3 to 5 minutes. Remove from heat. Stir in flour, sugar and nuts. Drop tablespoonfuls of dough 4 inches apart onto greased cookie sheets. Bake for 11 to 13 minutes, or until cookies bubble and are golden brown. Cool 1 minute on cookie sheet. Working quickly, remove and shape cookies over inverted small custard cups to form cups. Cool completely; remove from custard cups.

For each cup, spread 1 tablespoon melted chocolate on outside bottom and 1 inch up outside edge of each cooled cup. Refrigerate until chocolate is hardened, about 30 minutes. Just before serving, fill each cup with a large scoop of ice cream. If desired, drizzle with additional melted chocolate.

Makes about 2 dozen cookie cups

*A 6-ounce package of chocolate chips will coat 8 to 9 cookie cups, using 1 tablespoon melted chocolate per cup.

Note: Make the desired number of cookie cups. With remaining dough, bake as directed except shape cookies into cones or leave flat and serve as cookies.

TEA-TIME SANDWICH COOKIES

These delicate wafer cookies are paired together with a butter cream filling, forming a dainty treat for tea-time.

Cookies
2 cups all-purpose flour
1 cup LAND O LAKES® Butter,
   softened
⅓ cup whipping cream
   Granulated sugar, for dipping

Filling
¾ cup powdered sugar
¼ cup LAND O LAKES® Butter,
   softened
1 to 3 teaspoons milk
1 teaspoon vanilla or almond
   extract
   Food coloring (optional)

For cookies, in small mixer bowl, combine flour, butter and whipping cream. Beat at low speed, scraping bowl often, until well mixed, 2 to 3 minutes. Divide dough into thirds. Wrap in waxed paper. Refrigerate until firm, at least 2 hours.

Heat oven to 375°. Roll out each ⅓ of the dough on well-floured surface to ⅛-inch thickness. Cut out with 1½-inch round cookie cutters. Dip both sides of each cookie in granulated sugar. Place 1 inch apart on ungreased cookie sheets. Prick with fork. Bake for 6 to 9 minutes, or until slightly puffy but not brown. Cool 1 minute on cookie sheet; remove.

For filling, in small mixer bowl, combine powdered sugar, butter, milk and vanilla. Beat at medium speed, scraping bowl often, until smooth, 1 to 2 minutes. If desired, color filling. Spread ½ teaspoon of filling over bottoms of ½ of the cookies. Top with remaining cookies.

Makes about 4½ dozen cookies

PECAN TARTLETS

Bite-size shortbread tarts filled with caramel and pecans.

Tart Shells
½ cup LAND O LAKES® Butter,
   softened
½ cup granulated sugar
1 egg
1 teaspoon almond extract
1¾ cups all-purpose flour

Filling
1 cup powdered sugar
½ cup LAND O LAKES® Butter
⅓ cup dark corn syrup
1 cup chopped pecans
36 pecan halves

Heat oven to 400°. For tart shells, in large mixer bowl, combine all tart shell ingredients. Beat at medium speed, scraping bowl often, until mixture is crumbly, 2 to 3 minutes. Press 1 tablespoon of the mixture into ungreased cups of mini-muffin pans to form 36 (1¾- to 2-inch) shells. Bake for 7 to 10 minutes, or until very lightly browned. Remove from oven.

Reduce oven to 350°. For filling, in medium saucepan, combine powdered sugar, butter and corn syrup. Cook, stirring occasionally, over medium heat until mixture comes to a full boil, 4 to 5 minutes. Remove from heat; stir in chopped nuts. Spoon into baked shells. Top each with pecan half. Bake for 5 minutes. Cool completely; remove from pans.

Makes about 3 dozen tartlets

Tea-Time Sandwich Cookies

Strawberry Marzipan Bars

STRAWBERRY MARZIPAN BARS

*These European inspired bars have a very special flavor and texture that
makes them rich and extra elegant!*

Crust
1¼ cups all-purpose flour
⅓ cup firmly packed brown sugar
½ cup LAND O LAKES® Butter,
　softened

Filling
½ cup all-purpose flour
½ cup firmly packed brown sugar
¼ cup LAND O LAKES® Butter,
　softened
½ teaspoon almond extract
¾ cup strawberry preserves

Glaze
½ cup powdered sugar
1 to 2 teaspoons milk
½ teaspoon almond extract

Heat oven to 350°. For crust, in small mixer bowl, combine all crust ingredients. Beat at low speed, scraping bowl often, until mixture is crumbly, 1 to 2 minutes. Press on bottom of greased and floured 9-inch square baking pan. Bake for 15 to 20 minutes, or until edges are lightly browned.

For filling, in same mixer bowl, combine flour, brown sugar, butter and almond extract. Beat at low speed, scraping bowl often, until well mixed, 1 to 2 minutes. Spread preserves to within ¼ inch of edge of hot crust. Sprinkle filling mixture over preserves. Continue baking for 20 to 25 minutes, or until edges are lightly browned. Cool completely.

For glaze, in small bowl, stir together all glaze ingredients until smooth. Drizzle over cooled bars. Cut into bars.　　*Makes about 3 dozen bars*

EGGNOG SNICKERDOODLES

These eggnog snickerdoodles are a pleasant surprise.

Cookies
2¾ cups all-purpose flour
1½ cups sugar
　1 cup LAND O LAKES® Butter,
　　softened
　2 eggs
　2 teaspoons cream of tartar
　1 teaspoon baking soda

¼ teaspoon salt
½ teaspoon brandy extract
½ teaspoon rum extract

Sugar Mixture
¼ cup sugar or colored sugar
　1 teaspoon nutmeg

Heat oven to 400°. For cookies, in large mixer bowl, combine all cookie ingredients. Beat at low speed, scraping bowl often, until well mixed, 2 to 4 minutes.

For sugar mixture, in small bowl, stir together sugar and nutmeg. Shape rounded teaspoonfuls of dough into 1-inch balls; roll in sugar mixture. Place 2 inches apart on ungreased cookie sheets. Bake for 8 to 10 minutes, or until edges are lightly browned. Remove immediately.

Makes about 4 dozen cookies

ORANGE BUTTER CREAM SQUARES

This bar cookie combines two favorite flavors—orange and chocolate.

Crust
1¼ cups finely crushed chocolate
    wafer cookies
⅓ cup LAND O LAKES® Butter,
    softened

Filling
1½ cups powdered sugar
⅓ cup LAND O LAKES® Butter,
    softened
1 tablespoon milk
2 teaspoons grated orange peel
½ teaspoon vanilla

Glaze
1 tablespoon unsweetened cocoa
1 tablespoon LAND O LAKES®
    Butter, melted

For crust, in medium bowl, stir together cookie crumbs and butter. Press on bottom of ungreased 9-inch square baking pan. Refrigerate until firm, about 1 hour.

For filling, in small mixer bowl, combine all filling ingredients. Beat at medium speed, scraping bowl often, until light and fluffy, 3 to 4 minutes. Spread over crust.

For glaze, in small bowl, stir together cocoa and butter. Drizzle over filling. Refrigerate until firm, about 2 hours. Cut into bars. Store in refrigerator.

Makes about 2 dozen bars

PECAN PIE BARS

These bars are reminiscent of pecan pie.

Crust
2 cups all-purpose flour
½ cup powdered sugar
1 cup LAND O LAKES® Butter

Filling
1 can (14 ounces) sweetened
    condensed milk
1 egg
1 teaspoon vanilla
1 package (6 ounces) almond
    brickle bits
1 cup chopped pecans

Heat oven to 350°. For crust, in large bowl, combine flour and powdered sugar. Cut in butter until crumbly. Press firmly on bottom of ungreased 13×9×2-inch baking pan. Bake for 15 minutes.

For filling, in large bowl, stir together sweetened condensed milk, egg and vanilla. Stir in almond brickle bits and nuts. Spread evenly over hot crust. Continue baking for 25 to 28 minutes, or until golden brown. Cool; refrigerate until firm, 2 to 3 hours. Cut into bars. Store, covered, in refrigerator.

Makes about 3 dozen bars

Orange Butter Cream Squares

Double Mint Chocolate Cookies

DOUBLE MINT CHOCOLATE COOKIES

These puffy chocolate cookies are topped with a refreshing butter-mint frosting.

Cookies
- 2 cups granulated sugar
- 1 cup unsweetened cocoa
- 1 cup LAND O LAKES® Butter, softened
- 1 cup buttermilk or sour milk
- 1 cup water
- 2 eggs
- 2 teaspoons baking soda
- 1 teaspoon baking powder
- ½ teaspoon salt
- 1 teaspoon vanilla
- 4 cups all-purpose flour

Frosting
- 4 cups powdered sugar
- 1 cup LAND O LAKES® Butter, softened
- 1 teaspoon salt
- 2 tablespoons milk
- 2 teaspoons vanilla
- ½ teaspoon mint extract
- ½ cup crushed starlight peppermint candy

Heat oven to 400°. For cookies, in large mixer bowl, combine granulated sugar, cocoa, butter, buttermilk, water, eggs, baking soda, baking powder, salt and vanilla. Beat at low speed, scraping bowl often, until well mixed, 1 to 2 minutes. Stir in flour until well mixed, 3 to 4 minutes. Drop rounded teaspoonfuls of dough 2 inches apart onto greased cookie sheets. Bake for 7 to 9 minutes, or until top of cookie springs back when touched lightly in center. Remove immediately; cool completely.

For frosting, in small mixer bowl, combine powdered sugar, butter, salt, milk, vanilla and mint extract. Beat at medium speed, scraping bowl often, until light and fluffy, 2 to 3 minutes. Spread ½ tablespoonful of frosting on the top of each cookie. Sprinkle with candy.

Makes about 8 dozen cookies

CHERRY JEWELS

These pink molded cookies are buttery rich and very festive.

- 2¼ cups all-purpose flour
- ½ cup granulated sugar
- ⅔ cup LAND O LAKES® Butter, softened
- 1 egg
- ½ teaspoon ground nutmeg
- ¼ teaspoon salt
- ½ teaspoon brandy or rum extract
- ½ cup chopped maraschino cherries, drained
- Powdered sugar for sprinkling

Heat oven to 350°. In large mixer bowl, combine flour, granulated sugar, butter, egg, nutmeg, salt, brandy extract and cherries. Beat at low speed, scraping bowl often, until well mixed, 2 to 3 minutes. Shape rounded teaspoonfuls of dough into 1-inch balls. Place 2 inches apart on ungreased cookie sheets. Bake for 10 to 15 minutes, or until edges are lightly browned. Remove immediately; cool completely. Sprinkle with powdered sugar.

Makes about 3½ dozen cookies

MINT PASTRY WAFERS

A refreshing chocolate mint is sandwiched between two buttery tender wafers.

2 cups all-purpose flour
1 cup LAND O LAKES® Butter, softened
⅓ cup whipping cream or half and half

Sugar
24 thin chocolate mint wafers* or milk chocolate squares

In large mixer bowl, combine flour, butter and whipping cream. Beat at low speed, scraping bowl often, until well mixed, 1 to 2 minutes. Cover; refrigerate until firm enough to roll, 1 to 2 hours.

Heat oven to 400°. Roll out dough, ½ at a time, on well-floured surface, to ¼-inch thickness. Cut out with 2-inch round cookie cutters. Dip both sides of each cookie in sugar. Place ½ of the cookies 2 inches apart onto greased cookie sheets. Place 1 mint in center of each. Top with another cookie; press together around edges with fingers. Bake for 8 to 10 minutes, or until edges are very lightly browned. Cool 1 minute on cookie sheet; remove.

Makes about 2 dozen cookies

*Do not use chocolate fondant mints (cream filled mints).

BITS O'CHOCOLATE BANANA BARS

This moist banana bar, with pieces of chocolate, is made more special with a buttery rich frosting.

Bars
2¾ cups all-purpose flour
1¼ cups granulated sugar
1¼ cups bananas cut into ¼-inch slices (about 2 large)
¾ cup LAND O LAKES® Butter, softened
2 eggs
1¼ teaspoons baking powder
1¼ teaspoons baking soda
½ teaspoon salt

2 teaspoons vanilla
1 cup milk chocolate chips

Frosting
4 cups powdered sugar
½ cup LAND O LAKES® Butter, softened
¼ cup milk
2 teaspoons vanilla
Milk chocolate, shaved into small pieces

Heat oven to 350°. For bars, in large mixer bowl, combine flour, granulated sugar, bananas, butter, eggs, baking powder, baking soda, salt and vanilla. Beat at low speed, scraping bowl often, until well mixed, 2 to 3 minutes. Stir in chocolate chips. Spread into greased and floured 15×10×1-inch jelly-roll pan. Bake for 25 to 30 minutes, or until wooden pick inserted in center comes out clean. Cool completely.

For frosting, in small mixer bowl, combine powdered sugar, butter, milk and vanilla. Beat at medium speed, scraping bowl often, until light and fluffy, 2 to 3 minutes. Frost bars. Sprinkle shaved milk chocolate over tops. Cut into bars.

Makes about 4 dozen bars

Mint Pastry Wafers

Half-Hearted Valentine Cookies

HALF-HEARTED VALENTINE COOKIES

Peppermint flavoring complements chocolate-dipped butter cookies.

Cookies
¾ cup sugar
1 cup LAND O LAKES® Butter,
   softened
1 package (3 ounces) cream
   cheese, softened
1 egg

1 teaspoon peppermint extract
3 cups all-purpose flour

Glaze
1 cup semi-sweet real chocolate
   chips
¼ cup LAND O LAKES® Butter

For cookies, in large mixer bowl, combine sugar, butter, cream cheese, egg and peppermint extract. Beat at medium speed, scraping bowl often, until light and fluffy, 3 to 4 minutes. Add flour, continue beating until well mixed, 2 to 3 minutes. Divide dough into halves. Wrap in waxed paper. Refrigerate until firm, at least 2 hours.

Heat oven to 375°. Roll out dough on lightly floured surface to ¼-inch thickness. Cut out with floured heart-shaped cutters. Place 1 inch apart on ungreased cookie sheets. Bake for 7 to 10 minutes, or until edges are very lightly browned. Remove immediately; cool completely.

For glaze, in small saucepan, melt chocolate and butter, stirring occasionally, over low heat until melted, 4 to 6 minutes. Dip half of each heart into chocolate. Place on waxed paper-lined cookie sheet; refrigerate until chocolate is firm. Store, covered, in refrigerator.

Makes about 3½ dozen cookies

LEBKUCHEN SPICE SPRITZ COOKIES

The popular flavors of Lebkuchen cookies come alive in this easy-to-make spritz cookie.

Cookies
⅔ cup granulated sugar
1 cup LAND O LAKES® Butter,
   softened
1 egg
1 teaspoon ground cinnamon
1 teaspoon ground nutmeg
½ teaspoon ground allspice

¼ teaspoon ground cloves
2 teaspoons lemon juice
2 cups all-purpose flour

Glaze
1 cup powdered sugar
1 tablespoon milk
½ teaspoon vanilla

For cookies, in large mixer bowl, combine granulated sugar, butter, egg, cinnamon, nutmeg, allspice, cloves and lemon juice. Beat at medium speed, scraping bowl often, until mixture is light and fluffy, 2 to 3 minutes. Stir in flour until well mixed, 3 to 4 minutes. If dough is too soft, cover; refrigerate until firm enough to form cookies, 1 to 2 hours.

Heat oven to 400°. Place dough into cookie press; form desired shapes 1 inch apart on greased cookie sheets. Bake for 8 to 12 minutes, or until cookie edges are lightly browned. Remove immediately.

For glaze, in small bowl, stir together all glaze ingredients until smooth. Glaze can be drizzled on warm cookies or used with a pastry bag with decorator tip.

Makes about 5 dozen cookies

BRANDIED BUTTERY WREATHS

This rich, buttery cookie is delicately flavored with brandy and nutmeg.

Cookies
2¼ cups all-purpose flour
⅓ cup granulated sugar
⅔ cup LAND O LAKES® Butter, softened
1 egg
1 teaspoon ground nutmeg
¼ teaspoon salt
2 tablespoons grated orange peel
2 tablespoons brandy*
⅓ cup chopped maraschino cherries, drained

Glaze
1¼ cups powdered sugar
1 to 2 tablespoons milk
1 tablespoon brandy**
⅛ teaspoon ground nutmeg
Red and green maraschino cherries, cut into pieces or eighths and drained

Heat oven to 350° For cookies, in large mixer bowl, combine flour, granulated sugar, butter, egg, nutmeg, salt, orange peel and brandy. Beat at low speed, scraping bowl often, until well mixed, 1 to 2 minutes. Stir in cherries. Shape rounded teaspoonfuls of dough into 1-inch balls; form into 5-inch long strips. Shape strips into circles (wreaths), candy canes or leave as strips. Place 2 inches apart on greased cookie sheets. Bake for 8 to 12 minutes, or until edges are lightly browned. Remove immediately.

For glaze, in small bowl, stir together powdered sugar, milk, brandy and nutmeg until smooth. Frost warm cookies with glaze. Decorate with maraschino cherries.   *Makes about 2 dozen cookies*

*You may substitute 1 teaspoon brandy extract plus 2 tablespoons water for the 2 tablespoons brandy.
**You may substitute ½ teaspoon brandy extract plus 1 tablespoon water for the 1 tablespoon brandy.

Brandied Buttery Wreaths; Lebkuchen
Spice Spritz Cookies, page 91

IRISH MIST BROWNIES

A brownie layered with mint butter cream and drizzled with chocolate.

Brownies
½ cup LAND O LAKES® Butter
2 squares (1 ounce each)
   unsweetened chocolate
1 cup granulated sugar
¾ cup all-purpose flour
2 eggs

Frosting
2 cups powdered sugar
3 tablespoons LAND O LAKES®
   Butter, softened
1 package (3 ounces) cream
   cheese, softened
½ teaspoon peppermint extract
5 drops green food coloring
2 drops yellow food coloring
1 square (1 ounce) unsweetened
   chocolate, melted

Heat oven to 350°. For brownies, in medium saucepan, melt butter and chocolate, stirring constantly, over medium heat, 4 to 6 minutes. Stir in granulated sugar, flour and eggs until well mixed. Spread into greased 9-inch square baking pan. Bake for 25 to 30 minutes, or until brownies begin to pull away from sides of pan. Cool completely.

For frosting, in small mixer bowl, combine powdered sugar, butter, cream cheese, peppermint extract and food colorings. Beat at medium speed, scraping bowl often, until light and fluffy, 2 to 3 minutes. Spread over cooled bars. Drizzle melted chocolate over top. Cut into bars. Store, covered, in refrigerator.   *Makes about 2 dozen bars*

PIÑA COLADA COOKIES

*Inspired by the beverage of the same name, this easy drop cookie
combines pineapple, coconut and a hint of rum.*

Cookies
½ cup granulated sugar
⅓ cup LAND O LAKES® Butter,
   softened
2 eggs
⅓ cup pineapple preserves
½ teaspoon baking powder
½ teaspoon salt
½ teaspoon rum extract
1¾ cups all-purpose flour
¼ cup flaked coconut

Frosting
¾ cup powdered sugar
¼ cup LAND O LAKES® Butter,
   softened
1 teaspoon water
¼ teaspoon rum extract
   Toasted flaked coconut

Heat oven to 350°. For cookies, in large mixer bowl, combine granulated sugar, butter, eggs, preserves, baking powder, salt and rum extract. Beat at low speed, scraping bowl often, until well mixed, 1 to 2 minutes. Stir in flour and coconut until well mixed, 2 to 3 minutes. Drop rounded teaspoonfuls of dough 2 inches apart onto greased cookie sheets. Bake for 8 to 12 minutes, or until edges are lightly browned. Remove immediately. Cool completely.

For frosting, in small mixer bowl, combine powdered sugar, butter, water and rum extract. Beat at medium speed, scraping bowl often, until light and fluffy, 1 to 2 minutes. Spread over cooled cookies. Sprinkle tops with toasted coconut.   *Makes about 3 dozen cookies*

INDEX

Almond Brickle Sugar Cookies, 79
Almond Macaroon Bars, 44
Almond Shortbread Bars, 18
Apples
    Apple Pie Bars, 40
    Spice 'n' Easy Apple Raisin Bars, 44

Bananas
    Banana Cream Sandwich Cookies, 58
    Bits O'Chocolate Banana Bars, 88
Bar cookies
    Almond Macaroon Bars, 44
    Almond Shortbread Bars, 18
    Apple Pie Bars, 40
    Bits O'Chocolate Banana Bars, 88
    Buttery Caramel Crisps, 29
    Caramel Chocolate Pecan Bars, 43
    Caramel Rocky Road Bars, 22
    Cherry Date Sparkle Bars, 36
    Cherry Scotchies, 33
    Chocolate Meringue Peanut Squares, 68
    Citrus Pie Bars, 51
    Coconut Date Candy Squares, 43
    Crisp 'n' Crunchy Almond Coconut Bars, 36
    Frosted Honey Bars, 47
    Glazed Rum Raisin Bars, 52
    Glistening Cherry-Fig Bars, 17
    Granola Goody Bars, 13
    Honey Nut Chess Bars, 52
    Irish Mist Brownies, 94
    Jan Hagel, 48
    Layered Chocolate Butterscotch Bars, 6
    Lemon-Butter Snowbars, 71
    Mocha Almond Bars, 14
    Old-Fashioned Brownies, 26
    Old-World Raspberry Bars, 18
    Orange Butter Cream Squares, 84
    Orange Date Treasure Bars, 48
    Peanut Butter Chocolate Chip Bars, 30
    Pecan Pie Bars, 84
    Pineapple Cheesecake Bars, 51
    Rocky Road Fudge Brownies, 33
    Sour Cream Cherry Bars, 6

    Spice 'n' Easy Apple Raisin Bars, 44
    Strawberry Marzipan Bars, 83
    Strawberry Wonders, 39
    Sunny Lemon Oatmeal Bars, 47
    Teentime Dream Bars, 25
    Toasted Pecan Toffee Bars, 26
    Twist O'Lemon Cheesecakes, 39
Bits O'Chocolate Banana Bars, 88
Black Walnut Refrigerator Cookies, 68
Brandied Buttery Wreaths, 92
Butterscotch chips
    Buttery Butterscotch Cutouts, 72
    Caramel Chocolate Pecan Bars, 43
    Cherry Scotchies, 33
    Layered Chocolate Butterscotch Bars, 6
    Rocky Road Fudge Brownies, 33
Buttery Butterscotch Cutouts, 72
Buttery Caramel Crisps, 29
Buttery Jam Tarts, 25

Candy and Peanut Jumbles, 63
Caramel Chocolate Pecan Bars, 43
Caramel Rocky Road Bars, 22
Cherries
    Brandied Buttery Wreaths, 92
    Cherry Date Skillet Cookies, 13
    Cherry Date Sparkle Bars, 36
    Cherry Jewels, 87
    Cherry Scotchies, 33
    Glistening Cherry-Fig Bars, 17
    Sour Cream Cherry Bars, 6
Chocolate
    Bits O'Chocolate Banana Bars, 88
    Candy and Peanut Jumbles, 63
    Caramel Chocolate Pecan Bars, 43
    Caramel Rocky Road Bars, 22
    Chocolate Chunk Cookies, 30
    Chocolate Meringue Peanut Squares, 68
    Chocolate Pixies, 71
    Half-Hearted Valentine Cookies, 91
    Irish Mist Brownies, 94
    Lace Cookie Cups with Ice Cream, 79
    Layered Chocolate Butterscotch Bars, 6
    Mint Pastry Wafers, 88
    Peanut Butter Chocolate Chip Bars, 30
    Rocky Road Fudge Brownies, 33
    Teddy Bear Cookies, 29
    Teentime Dream Bars, 25
    Toasted Pecan Toffee Bars, 26

Cinnamon Raisin Oatmeal Cookies, 72
Cinnamon Sugar Crispies, 9
Citrus Pie Bars, 51
Cocoa
    Double Mint Chocolate Cookies, 87
    Old-Fashioned Brownies, 26
    Orange Butter Cream Squares, 84
Coconut
    Almond Macaroon Bars, 44
    Buttery Caramel Crisps, 29
    Cherry Date Skillet Cookies, 13
    Cherry Date Sparkle Bars, 36
    Cherry Scotchies, 33
    Citrus Pie Bars, 51
    Coconut Date Candy Squares, 43
    Coconut Snowdrops, 14
    Cookie Jar Cookies, 22
    Crisp 'n' Crunchy Almond Coconut Bars, 36
    Layered Chocolate Butterscotch Bars, 6
    Lemon Doodles, 10
    Piña Colada Cookies, 94
    Strawberry Wonders, 39
    Swedish Coconut Cookies, 9
    Teentime Dream Bars, 25
    Tropical Orange Coconut Drops, 10
Cookie Jar Cookies, 22
Cornish Biscuit Cookies, 64
Country Sour Cream Cookies, 57
Cream cheese
    Frosted Honey Bars, 47
    Half-Hearted Valentine Cookies, 91
    Irish Mist Brownies, 94
    Pineapple Cheesecake Bars, 51
    Twist O'Lemon Cheesecakes, 39
Crisp 'n' Crunchy Almond Coconut Bars, 36

Dates
    Cherry Date Skillet Cookies, 13
    Cherry Date Sparkle Bars, 36
    Coconut Date Candy Squares, 43
    Orange Date Treasure Bars, 48
Double Mint Chocolate Cookies, 87
Drop cookies
    Candy and Peanut Jumbles, 63
    Chocolate Chunk Cookies, 30
    Cinnamon Raisin Oatmeal Cookies, 72
    Coconut Snowdrops, 14
    Cookie Jar Cookies, 22
    Cornish Biscuit Cookies, 64
    Double Mint Chocolate Cookies, 87
    Honey 'n' Spice Cookies, 63

continued
    Lace Cookie Cups with Ice
      Cream, 79
    Lemon Doodles, 10
    Maple Raisin Cookies, 64
    Peanut Buttery Cookies, 57
    Piña Colada Cookies, 94
    Sour Cream Brown Butter
      Cookies, 75
    Tropical Orange Coconut
      Drops, 10

Eggnog Snickerdoodles, 83

Favorite Butter Cookies, 61
Fig Bars, Glistening Cherry-, 17
Frosted Honey Bars, 47
Fruit Filled Thumbprints, 56

Glazed Rum Raisin Bars, 52
Glistening Cherry-Fig Bars, 17
Granola Goody Bars, 13

Half-Hearted Valentine Cookies, 91
Honey
    Frosted Honey Bars, 47
    Granola Goody Bars, 13
    Honey 'n' Spice Cookies, 63
    Honey Nut Chess Bars, 52
    Honey of a Cookie, 67

Irish Mist Brownies, 94

Jan Hagel, 48

Lace Cookie Cups with Ice Cream,
    79
Layered Chocolate Butterscotch
    Bars, 6
Lebkuchen Spice Spritz Cookies,
    91
Lemon
    Citrus Pie Bars, 51
    Lemon-Butter Snowbars, 71
    Lemon Doodles, 10
    Lemon Meltaways, 56
    Lemon-Nut Cookies, 75
    Sunny Lemon Oatmeal Bars, 47
    Twist O'Lemon Cheesecakes, 39

Maple Raisin Cookies, 64
Marshmallows
    Buttery Caramel Crisps, 29
    Caramel Rocky Road Bars, 22
    Rocky Road Fudge Brownies, 33
Mint
    Double Mint Chocolate
      Cookies, 87
    Half-Hearted Valentine Cookies,
      91

Irish Mist Brownies, 94
Mint Pastry Wafers, 88
Mocha Almond Bars, 14
Molasses Cookies, Spiced, 67

Oats
    Candy and Peanut Jumbles, 63
    Caramel Rocky Road Bars, 22
    Cinnamon Raisin Oatmeal
      Cookies, 72
    Cookie Jar Cookies, 22
    Spice 'n' Easy Apple Raisin Bars,
      44
    Strawberry Wonders, 39
    Sunny Lemon Oatmeal Bars, 47
Old-Fashioned Brownies, 26
Old-Fashioned Butter Cookies, 58
Old-World Raspberry Bars, 18
Orange
    Brandied Buttery Wreaths, 92
    Favorite Butter Cookies, 61
    Honey 'n' Spice Cookies, 63
    Orange Butter Cream Squares,
      84
    Orange Date Treasure Bars, 48
    Tropical Orange Coconut
      Drops, 10

Peanut butter
    Peanut Butter Chocolate Chip
      Bars, 30
    Teentime Dream Bars, 25
Peanut Buttery Cookies, 57
Peanuts
    Candy and Peanut Jumbles, 63
    Caramel Rocky Road Bars, 22
    Chocolate Meringue Peanut
      Squares, 68
    Layered Chocolate Butterscotch
      Bars, 6
    Peanut Butter Chocolate Chip
      Bars, 30
    Peanut Buttery Cookies, 57
    Rocky Road Fudge Brownies, 33
Pecan Pie Bars, 84
Pecan Tartlets, 80
Piña Colada Cookies, 94
Pineapple Cheesecake Bars, 51
Preserves
    Buttery Jam Tarts, 25
    Fruit Filled Thumbprints, 56
    Old-World Raspberry Bars, 18
    Piña Colada Cookies, 94
    Strawberry Marzipan Bars, 83
    Strawberry Wonders, 39

Raisins
    Cinnamon Raisin Oatmeal
      Cookies, 72
    Cornish Biscuit Cookies, 64

Glazed Rum Raisin Bars, 52
Granola Goody Bars, 13
Maple Raisin Cookies, 64
Spice 'n' Easy Apple Raisin Bars,
    44
Refrigerator cookies
    Black Walnut Refrigerator
      Cookies, 68
    Swedish Coconut Cookies, 9
Rocky Road Fudge Brownies, 33
Rolled cookies
    Buttery Butterscotch Cutouts,
      72
    Buttery Jam Tarts, 25
    Country Sour Cream Cookies, 57
    Favorite Butter Cookies, 61
    Half-Hearted Valentine Cookies,
      91
    Mint Pastry Wafers, 88
    Tea-Time Sandwich Cookies, 80

Shaped cookies
    Almond Brickle Sugar Cookies,
      79
    Banana Cream Sandwich
      Cookies, 58
    Brandied Buttery Wreaths, 92
    Cherry Date Skillet Cookies, 13
    Cherry Jewels, 87
    Chocolate Pixies, 71
    Cinnamon Sugar Crispies, 9
    Eggnog Snickerdoodles, 83
    Fruit Filled Thumbprints, 56
    Honey of a Cookie, 67
    Lace Cookie Cups with Ice
      Cream, 79
    Lebkuchen Spice Spritz
      Cookies, 91
    Lemon Meltaways, 56
    Lemon-Nut Cookies, 75
    Old-Fashioned Butter Cookies,
      58
    Pecan Tartlets, 80
    Snowball Cookies, 17
    Spiced Molasses Cookies, 67
    Teddy Bear Cookies, 29
Snowball Cookies, 17
Spice 'n' Easy Apple Raisin Bars, 44
Spiced Molasses Cookies, 67
Strawberry Marzipan Bars, 83
Strawberry Wonders, 39
Sunny Lemon Oatmeal Bars, 47
Swedish Coconut Cookies, 9

Tea-Time Sandwich Cookies, 80
Teddy Bear Cookies, 29
Teentime Dream Bars, 25
Toasted Pecan Toffee Bars, 26
Tropical Orange Coconut Drops, 10
Twist O'Lemon Cheesecakes, 39

The cookie experts from Land O'Lakes invite you to try their delicious assortment of melt-in-your-mouth cookies. The LAND O LAKES® COOKIE COLLECTION is a must if you love cookies. Each bar cookie, filled cookie, holiday cookie, drop cookie, decorated cookie and sophisticated cookie has been carefully created and tested by the Land O'Lakes Test Kitchens. And you can be sure the buttery goodness of each LAND O LAKES® recipe makes every homemade cookie a tasty treat.

ISBN 0-517-03307-0

9 780517 033074   90000

Crescent Books
Distributed by Outlet Book Company, Inc.
A Random House Company